The LOVE There That's SLEEPING

The LOVE There That's SLEEPING

The Art and Spirituality of George Harrison

Dale C. Allison Jr.

continuum
NEW YORK • LONDON

Copyright © 2006 by Dale C. Allison Jr.

All rights reserved. No part of this book may be reproduced, stored in a retrieval system, or transmitted in any form or by any means, electronic, mechanical, including photocopying, recording, or otherwise, without the written permission of the publisher.

The Continuum International Publishing Group,
80 Maiden Lane, New York, NY 10038

The Continuum International Publishing Group Ltd,
The Tower Building, 11 York Road, London SE1 7NX

Cover art: George Harrison (1943–2001) of The Beatles leaves the bus in Plymouth during the location filming of "Magical Mystery Tour," 1967. (Photo by Keystone/Hulton Archive/Getty Images)

Cover design: Wesley Hoke

Library of Congress Cataloging-in-Publication Data

Allison, Dale C.
  The love there that's sleeping : the art and spirituality of George Harrison / Dale C. Allison, Jr.
    p. cm.
  Includes bibliographical references.
  "The songs of George Harrison : an annotated list and index": p.
  ISBN-13: 978-0-8264-2756-4 (hardcover)
  ISBN-10: 0-8264-2756-1 (hardcover)
  ISBN-13: 978-0-8264-1917-0 (paperback)
  ISBN-10: 0-8264-1917-8 (paperback)
  1. Harrison, George, 1943-2001—Religion. 2. Harrison, George, 1943-2001—Criticism and interpretation. 3. Rock music—Religious aspects. I. Title.
  ML420.H167A75 2006
  782.42166092—dc22
                    2006019631

06 07 08 09 10 11   10 9 8 7 6 5 4 3 2 1

For
Jeff Bryant
My Fellow DJ

Contents

1. Introduction   1
2. God, God, God
   THEOLOGY   6
3. Use My Body Like a Car
   HUMAN NATURE   24
4. Chanting the Name of the Lord
   ESTABLISHED RELIGIONS   40
5. The Material World
   OUR PREDICAMENT   61
6. The Art of Dying
   DEATH AND REINCARNATION   78
7. Brainwashed
   HUMAN FOLLY   95
8. The Love There That's Sleeping
   SALVATION   114
9. Thanks for the Pepperoni
   AN APPRECIATION   132

The Songs of George Harrison
AN ANNOTATED LIST AND INDEX   135

Index   161

Introduction

I've been surprised by how many people, upon learning that I'm writing a book on George Harrison, have responded by saying that he is their favorite Beatle. I wonder whether he has always been their favorite, or whether the passing of the years has brought added appreciation. Whatever the truth may be for others, my favoritism goes back to the beginning.

I was only eight years old when my father, on a Sunday evening in 1964, called me up from playing Ping-Pong in our basement to witness the spectacle of The Beatles on *Ed Sullivan*. I don't recall what I then thought. (My parents laughed.) But I do remember that one afternoon, a few months later, four kids in my neighborhood in Wichita, Kansas, gave a Beatles concert for their mothers. Three of us strummed toy guitars while another banged the top of an overturned plastic bucket. Yet a fifth youngster, out of sight in the nearby garage, played a 45 rpm record. "I Want To Hold Your Hand" was on one side, "I Saw Her Standing There" on the other. I enacted the part of George, which meant I kept my mouth shut and pretended I knew what to do with a guitar, which I most certainly did not.

I don't recall whether I decided to play the part of George, or whether someone else made that decision for me. In the years to come, however, my interest in and partiality for George were firmly established, in part because I often preferred his sound to that of his companions. My favorite song on *The Beatles (The White Album)* has always been "While My Guitar Gently Weeps," which George wrote with Eric Clapton; and surely George's "Something" and "Here Comes The Sun" can lay decent claim to being the best offerings on *Abbey Road*, an album that can in turn lay decent claim to being The Beatles' best. In short, George produced some of the finest and most memorable music in The Beatles' canon.

After The Beatles disbanded and George released his first solo album, *All Things Must Pass* (1970), my appreciation for George increased. It has not subsided since. I remember the very first time I heard "My Sweet Lord" on the radio, and how much I enjoyed it; and I equally recall, more than thirty years later, anticipating the posthumous release of *Brainwashed* and fretting that I might be disappointed—which in the event I was not: it is excellent all the way through. To the end, George had a real knack for writing first-rate popular music. That the post-Beatle George is the favorite musician of one of my musically talented teenage sons is no mystery to me.

But why write a book on George?[1] There are many good reasons. He was a member of the foremost popular rock-and-roll band in history, a band for which the public still seems to have an insatiable appetite. Later on, during the 1970s and 1980s, he had a fair string of hits on his own and then with The Traveling Wilburys. He was sufficiently accomplished as a guitarist, especially at the slide—Eric Clapton once called him "a fantastic slide player"—that *Rolling Stone* magazine put him at number twenty-one in its list of "The 100 Greatest Guitarists of All Time," and, in 2003, his "Marwa Blues" won a posthumous Grammy for best pop instrumental performance. George also helped popularize sitarist Ravi Shankar and Indian music in the West, as well as other things eastern. Beyond the music scene, Harrison was a successful movie producer, having worked on, among other projects, Monty Python's riotous *Life of Brian* and Terry Gilliam's charming *Time Bandits*.

However noteworthy such popular culture facts might make him to others, I am myself interested in George because his songs regularly feature religious lyrics of substance. George in fact pioneered making mainstream rock a vehicle for religious convictions. In this respect he is the forerunner of subsequent bands such as U2 and Creed. He often, to be sure, suffered criticism for being didactic or preachy. Over the years, reviewers have often either exhibited an anxious disinclination to say much about his evangelistic lyrics or showed a condescending tendency to dismiss them. His devotional language was not their language. They regularly thought him sanctimonious and full of irrelevant religious platitudes.

From my point of view, however, his religious bent, so unfashionable in certain quarters, is not only noble but also his most interesting trait. Much popular music is at best vacuous, and it is a relief when we run across a talented performer with enough maturity and integrity to sing about more than just holding hands or similar trifles. George should be admired for having something distinctive to say, and for saying it knowing that many would not understand, and that those who would understand might not be sympathetic. He had the courage of his convictions to sing to the public what he sang to himself in his heart.

Although the introverted and introspective George was sometimes called the "quiet Beatle"—a tag he didn't like—he in fact had a great deal to say, especially about his religious faith. Being myself incurably religious from an early age, I have long been intrigued by his pilgrimage, which took him from Liverpool Roman Catholicism to a brand of philosophical Hinduism. Although he ended up seeing the world through Hindu eyes whereas I have ended up seeing it through Christian eyes, we often see things in a similar way. The conjunction creates sympathy and likewise has given me much to ponder. Furthermore, part of the value of listening to George is that one is doing far more than listening to a pop musician. George doesn't just speak for himself: he also speaks on behalf of a rich religious tradition. His words, then, can be and often are larger than himself, their wisdom wiser than their mouthpiece.

My goal in this book is to interpret those words, to sort through George's musical corpus, through its mixed bag of fragmentary feelings, religious poetry, secular love songs, perceptions of the world, and anxieties about life, and more or less to systematize, in the light of his biography, his understanding of what matters most. In short, this is a book about George's religious sentiments as they surface in his songs.

Unfortunately, my knowledge of George is entirely secondhand. It comes to me indirectly, through records, books, and videos. I have never, in one sense, known him at all. He is like the other so-called celebrities who fill up the empty spaces in our lives, people we know without knowing. In truth, one suspects that this lack of authentic familiarity is generally a very good thing. We lose little, and sometimes even gain something, by not being acquainted firsthand with many celebrities.

But I prefer to think that George was different. I imagine that he was, unlike so many famous people, a genuinely interesting person outside of the public spotlight, someone with whom I might well have enjoyed conversing. I am much taken by his comment that "I'm really quite simple. I don't want to be in the [music] business full-time, because I'm a gardener. I plant flowers and watch them grow. I don't go out to clubs and party. I stay at home and watch the river flow."[2] These humble words, with their allusion to Bob Dylan, are wonderful in that they come from a former Beatle, from a man who at one time had the whole world at his feet. He'd been there and done that, and was sensible enough to know that having one's own feet in the soil of one's own garden was a much better circumstance.

George's human decency and generous character are evident on the DVD of *The Concert For George* (2003). This event, held at London's Royal Albert Hall on the first anniversary of George's death, features Joe Brown, Eric Clapton, Jeff Lynne, Paul McCartney, Tom Petty, Anoushka Shankar, and Ringo Starr, among others, offering reminiscences and playing music in George's honor. Watching the show, one cannot escape the impression that George was, even to those who knew him, a bit larger than life: the performers are obviously celebrating not just his music but also the man himself. Whether or not George's shade, when looking down, felt a bit discomfited by all the admiring attention, those who paid tribute thought him, despite his foibles and failures, worthy. I similarly believe that his music is worthy of the sort of attention it receives in the following pages.

This is the first book I have written that every member of my immediate family has wanted to read, and they have all helped me with the manuscript. So to my ever-supportive and wonderful wife, Kris, and to my remarkable three children, Emily, Andrew, and John, thanks for everything. John in particular helped with some of the research. Gratitude also goes to Henry Carrigan, of T & T Clark International, for first raising with me the possibility of doing this book, and for his confidence in my ability to stray so far from my usual areas of expertise. Execution of the project has been gratifying. A few friends have also helped me with one or more chapters: Kathy Anderson, Jeff Bryant, Chris Kettler, Joel Marcus.

I dedicate this book to Jeff Bryant, my friend from so far back. I often recall, Jeff, the good old days, before we felt the full weight of the world, when we talked St. Louis Cardinals baseball and built model rockets, played spades and listened to rock-and-roll music, shot hoops and gossiped about school. My father was always so proud of the good company I kept as a youngster, and in retrospect I feel the same way. Ever since we left college together, you have kept me well supplied with popular music when I was preoccupied elsewhere. As inadequate exchange for all the tapes thoughtfully mailed to me over the years, tapes that have given me so much enjoyment, here's a book. I hope you like it.

Notes

1. Helpful biographies include Alan Clayson, *George Harrison* (rev. ed.; London: Sanctuary, 2001); Joshua M. Greene, *Here Comes the Sun: The Spiritual and Musical Journey of George Harrison* (Hoboken, NJ: John Wiley & Sons, 2006); and Elliot J. Huntley, *Mystical One: George Harrison after the Break-up of The Beatles* (Toronto: Guernica, 2004). Harrison's own autobiographical account, *I, Me, Mine* (San Francisco: Chronicle Books, 2002), is brief and spotty and covers only the first half of his life. The finest analysis of George's music, which happily is almost comprehensive, is Simon Leng, *The Music of George Harrison: While My Guitar Gently Weeps* (London: Fire Fly, 2003).

2. This is from an Associated Press release from 1989, in which George attempts to describe his relationship with Paul McCartney.

God, God, God

THEOLOGY

*T*wo songs aptly flank George Harrison's solo career. The first is "My Sweet Lord," the infectious hit from his earliest post-Beatle album, *All Things Must Pass*.[1] The other, unfortunately less well known, is "Brainwashed," the delightful last entry on George's final CD of the same name. Each song is an emotionally charged expression of religious devotion—a prayer addressed to the Deity. When we listen, the words are not directed firstly at us; we are instead overhearing George converse with his God.

In "My Sweet Lord," the singer repeatedly invokes God as "Lord" and expresses his fervent desire to see and know the Supreme Being. The strong, gospel-like chorus, which repeats his plea again and again, reinforces Harrison's earnestness. Although the song is buoyant, it remains a bit plaintive, for George fears that the full gratification of his religious yearning will take more time rather than less.

In "Brainwashed," whose infectious refrain repeats "God, God, God" a full sixteen times, George pleads with his Lord to lead humanity out of the predicament in which it is mired. Believing that our teachers and leaders have brainwashed us so that we ignorantly pour concrete, pursue wealth, and seek contentment in computers, mobile phones, and satellites, George prays that we might instead be brainwashed by God. The Divinity he thus implores to remake us doesn't just confer wisdom and knowledge but also bestows bliss and is like a lover. As with "My Sweet Lord," the passion is ardent, the longing sincere. George is God-intoxicated.

The religious infatuation on display at both the beginning and end of George's solo career typifies the whole. 1975's *Extra Texture: Read All About It*—the title, although obviously a play on the call of the old newspaper sellers: "Extra, extra, read all about it!," remains enigmatic—is, in fact, the sole Harrison album that fails to make any positive theological statements. The circumstance is so novel and surprising as to call for some explanation; and it is unlikely to be a coincidence that this album also features what is by far George's most depressing song, the dark and gloomy "Grey Cloudy Lies." This relentlessly despondent offering, which recalls a time when the singer put a pistol to his head, documents the dreadful temptation to commit suicide. George himself wrote that this song was the product of what he called his "naughty years" (the mid-seventies) when he drank too much, used cocaine, and finally separated from Pattie Boyd, his first wife.[2] In a 1975 interview, he said, "Compared to what I should be, I'm a heathen."[3] It is natural to guess that the absence of God from the lyrics of *Extra Texture* mirrors a perceived absence of God in George's personal life; and the emptiness was so intensely troubling that it fostered, at least momentarily, thoughts of taking his own life.

Consistent with this guess is that, in other songs on *Extra Texture*, George abandons his earlier religious content for ambiguity. In "World of Stone," for instance, he tells others that, if they are wise, they will not follow his example. He sings that he is far from home and far from "OM," which is his way of expressing his remoteness from both God and his own ideals. (*Bhagavad-Gita* 8:13 identifies the sound "OM" with Brahman and promises that chanting it with attention on one's deathbed will lead one to "the highest goal." In 10:25, Krishna identifies his transcendental self with "OM" and construes chanting the holy names—the act of "japa"—as an act of sacrifice.) The disparity between this confused melancholy and the confident religious advocacy on *All Things Must Pass* and *Living In The Material World* is remarkable. All pontifical pronouncements have ceased. George has come to doubt what matters to him most.

In the mellow "The Answer's At The End," also on *Extra Texture*, George observes that the language of flowers is more excellent than human speech, by which he means to convey his inability to figure out rationally what has happened to him. When he goes on to confess that the most difficult thing to reach is what's in the heart, he is surely talking about his inability to find God, who for him dwells, above all, inside the human being. No longer playing the evangelist, he concedes that life is an enigma, a great mystery to which he no longer has the answers, and further that, whatever the answers turn out to be, we won't know them until the end. Only death will reveal whether George has been deceived or not, whether his religious beliefs have been true or false. His faith has ceased to be his consoling certainty. It is now a question.

The absence of constructive theology from *Extra Texture*, whatever the biographical explanation, remains the anomaly. On *Thirty-Three & 1/3*, the album immediately following *Extra Texture*, the old religion, although muted a bit, is back, and it never leaves. This album includes "Dear One," in which George informs us that his mind is now at rest, for once again God is near him. George has been blessed. In response, he sings of his love for God, who is no longer silent or passive, and who knows how George feels and hearkens to him.

The rest of Harrison's musical corpus does nothing but add testimony to his belief in God's surpassing importance, an importance that relativizes everything else. Human beings, he tells us again and again, really need nothing except the Lord who is in all of us. "Life Itself," on *Somewhere In England*, even goes so far as to say, quite simply, that God is "all that is real." The implication is that everything else is somehow not real, even illusory. This is why George, playing martyr in his imagination, can even declare that God is the one for whom he would die. The fascinating but little-known "Sat Singing," to which we shall soon return, embodies the same conviction. Here George professes that the bliss of God is such that, when his time to die comes, he will happily say good-bye to this world. He will find his life by losing it and dwell forever in God's company.

Perhaps the most touching expression of George's religious passion appears on his highly successful 1987 album, *Cloud Nine*. The lyrics, for the most part, are much less serious than those of his previous endeavors. The whole production seems to have been above all an excuse for an old rocker to have some fun and try for a few more hits. On the latter count he certainly succeeded. "Got My Mind Set On You" went to number one on the U.S. charts, and the album sold a million copies even though George didn't tour to support it.

The jacket itself intimates the popular aim and content. Unlike some of the somber portraits on earlier album covers, *Cloud Nine* features a beaming George holding his guitar, his wide smile showing his bright white teeth. Lord Krishna is nowhere in sight. Even before hearing a note, then, our eyes lead our ears to anticipate a good time. We are not disappointed. With guest musicians Elton John tinkling the piano and Eric Clapton strumming his guitar, George here creates a marketable, thoroughly enjoyable pop sound. "When We Was Fab"—largely a mixture of old Beatle sounds—and "Got My Mind Set On You"—a remake of an obscure rhythm and blues song from James Ray (one of George's favorites)—were clearly designed for radio play, which they received. And the good-humored "Wreck Of The Hesperus" (named after Longfellow's epic poem), in which a genial George has a fine time mocking himself as an aged rocker—he was forty-four at the time—says not one word about death or God.

And yet in the middle of all this pop indulgence and lack of religious assertion is "Fish On The Sand." Musically Beatlesque, it is a complaint that, although God is in the sun and the moon and close to everyone, George nonetheless feels empty and alone. He frets that God has somehow gone away, that God no longer has "a hold" on him. Despite his fervent need and love for God, the Divinity has become an absence instead of a presence.

Like Tevye in *Fiddler On The Roof*, George doesn't deny his experience but is honest about his vexatious thoughts and feelings, and so he complains. He is in pain and tired. God has seemingly been playing hide-and-seek, and George, exasperated, has finally given up the game.

His arresting, short-tempered complaint is especially surprising after the transcendent bliss recorded earlier in "Sat Singing." George doesn't feel God within, and he unexpectedly places the blame not on himself but upon his Lord, who loves him so much. George is nonplussed.

The singer's devotion is such, however, that the complaint from the dark night of his soul can't sustain itself for long. The sinister doubt and despair of *Extra Texture* don't return; there is no gun at George's head. On the contrary, as soon as he grumbles his objection, he immediately goes on to acknowledge that, without God, he is not really a man but more "like a fish on the sand." Harrison was a Pisces, born on February 25, and in "Fish On The Sand" he inserts himself into the old saying about a fish out of water. Apart from the Supreme Reality, he is useless, unable to do anything; he is just like a fish expiring on dry land. So although George feels far from his God, he cannot deny God's incomparable value, and he knows that he will find meaning nowhere else. Despite, then, his current emptiness and frustration, religious faith remains. This is why, in "Fish On The Sand," in contrast to the songs on *Extra Texture*, George speaks not to us but to his God: the I-Thou relationship is, notwithstanding the existential void, intact.

But who or what is George's God? As we shall see later, George is a theistic Hindu, and he is quite clear about his devotion to Lord Krishna. Throughout most of his music, however, he prefers to use the simple and unelaborated word, "God." This typical lack of amplification is a calculated strategy. For George agrees with the Hindu philosophy known as neo-Vedanta, according to which the one divine reality goes under different names among the different faiths: the major religions of the world ultimately witness to the same transcendent reality. This is why George usually, if not always, leaves God unnamed, so that his listeners can find their own theology in his music. He wants to sing of the Supreme Soul in such a way that, for example, Christians and Sufis as well as Hindus can identify their God with his God.

Despite the sometimes studied ambiguity, George's music does make a number of properly theological statements, that is, assertions about the nature of the Divinity. One is that the Supreme Being is personal. This is not an idea we should take for granted. It's possible to think of God as an impersonal force, or simply to identify God with all that exists. Furthermore, George began his pilgrimage into Hinduism by heeding Maharishi Mahesh Yogi, the proponent of Transcendental Meditation; George later became interested in and visited Sathya Sai Baba, the great wonder-worker of twentieth-century India (he is mentioned in "Rocking Chair In Hawaii," and George sports a Sai Baba face pin inside the cover of *Extra Texture*); and George paid great heed to the writings of Swami Prabhavananda, who was so influential in spreading so-called Vedanta, a sophisticated philosophical form of Hinduism, throughout the West. The association with these three modern gurus is important because they tended to align themselves with the great Shankara, the ninth-century Hindu philosopher; and Shankara, as the chief proponent of the school of thought known as Advaita Vedanta, urged that all reality derives from a single divine source, Brahman, the impersonal, transcendent absolute, and that all plurality and differentiation are really an illusion. George believed this, believed in *advaita*, the principle of nonduality.

Notwithstanding George's undoubted monism, it surfaces only occasionally in his music. Just as later Hindu thinkers often sought to mix the personal and impersonal, so too did George: he said plainly enough that the Supreme Being has personal as well as impersonal aspects.[4] In his lyrics, moreover, the former trumps the latter. The overwhelming impression left by George's music is not that God is impersonal Brahman but, in the spirit of the *Bhagavad-Gita*, that God is a personal reality. Not only does George petition God for this and for that, but he also offers heartfelt thanksgiving, as in "Pure Smokey," where he gives thanks for each new day, or in "Unknown Delight," where he returns thanks to God for the gift of his son, Dhani.

The personal nature of the Deity is most evident in George's persistent association of the Transcendent with love. For him, as for the New Testament's First Epistle of John, "God is love." The touching "Looking For My Life," which tells of George's narrow escape from the knife of a madman at the end of 1999, addresses God simply as "Love"; and "Your Love Is Forever," from the previous decade, reckons God's love to be the supreme value, to which nothing is comparable. George is a proponent of what Hindus call *bhakti*, which so emphasizes religious devotion and love of God. Its faithful practice puts one in touch with a transcendent love that, as in "If You Believe" on *George Harrison*, flows all around us.

This divine love is, for George, relational: It invites a response, a reciprocal love. And this is the one thing needful. As George once said in an interview, "Krishna is actually a person who is the Lord and who will also appear . . . when there is that love, that bhakti. You can't understand the first thing about God unless you love Him."[5] So George sings to his "sweet Lord," whom he calls "Dear One" or imagines as the "lover that we miss." This mutual, loving relationship between the Divine and the human means that sometimes it is impossible to tell whether a song is about George's love for a woman or about his love for God. Clearly most of his compositions for The Beatles, including "Something," have no theological dimension to them—the one exception being "Long Long Long" on *The Beatles (The White Album)*; that is indeed about George's longing for the Deity. There are also secular love songs from his post-Beatles period. "Ooh Baby (You Know That I Love You)," "Soft Touch," and "Dark Sweet Lady" are not, it goes without saying, religious testimonials.

Other songs are of unclear import; we do not know whether they are meditations upon human love or religious love. This is true, for example, of "Wake Up My Love" (although I'm inclined to think it religious). In the end, however, it doesn't much matter. The one sort of love so much stands for the other in George's mind that the two sorts of love songs have become one. He said this in 1977: "All individual love between one person loving another, or loving this, that, or the other, is all small parts or small examples [*sic*] of that one universal love. It's all God. . . . Singing to the Lord or an individual is, in [a] way, the same. I've done that consciously in some songs."[6]

But some compositions, even though they are not explicitly religious and could be heard by careless listeners as ordinary love songs, are unambiguous, such as "Love Comes To Everyone" and "Life Itself," and the delightful if musically simple "Blow Away." The latter, a tribute to the power of positive thinking, is not about finding happiness through human love. The giveaway is the line in which the singer tells us that he closed his eyes, after which his head filled with light: this is for George religious language.

Notwithstanding the prominence of divine love in George's music, one remains disappointed that its meaning is offered as self-evident. He never really lets us know what it means to affirm that God loves us.

The answer is far from obvious. The world has always been filled to overflowing with woe and misery. Leukemia eats little children; tsunamis ravage busy villages; and some are thrown into the world with freakish birth defects. So what sense does it make, given brutal experience, to assert that the power behind the universe is loving? The theologians, eastern and western, have of course offered their reflections, and some of what they have said is helpful. But the point is that it requires only the least experience and reflection to confront the problem of evil. It is disappointing that someone as perceptive and serious as George, who was open-eyed about and concerned for the world's evils—as the Concert for Bangladesh[7] and his later public support for the Romanian Angels Appeal demonstrate—never bothered to share publicly his musings on this troubling topic.

Also disappointing is George's failure to spell out in detail what human love of the divine should look like, and what the implications for, say, ethics might be. This is perhaps from one point of view a carry-over from his days as a Beatle. Whatever John Lennon meant by it, and whether he was being serious or sarcastic when he preached to the world, "All You Need Is Love," and then added, "it's easy," he offered no illustration of what he was talking about. Was Lennon telling us to be kind? Were we being enjoined to feel a particular way? Or were we being summoned to concrete deeds of unselfish service? And will this "love," whatever it may be, truly overcome evil without itself acting in nonloving ways, as defense of innocent victims often seems to necessitate? Whatever Lennon did or did not think about such questions, he remained mute, and his famous song has rightly drawn cynical criticism. Similarly, George happily sings about loving God without telling us what is involved. Never once do we hear that we should do such-and-such because God loves human beings. Perhaps this lacuna partly reflects the circumstance that he wrote his religious love songs in the first instance for himself, so that he might sing them to God. They were, we may think, never intended to persuade anyone else of anything.

What else does George have to say about God? A number of divine attributes show up in George's music—God's knowledge of everything, God's presence everywhere, and God's eternal nature, for instance—but it is notable that the lyricist never passes beyond bare assertion. He says this and he says that about God, but he nowhere elaborates. This puzzles even more than his singing about love, for our age is characterized by serious, widespread religious doubt, much of it seemingly well-founded. We come after Feuerbach, Marx, Nietzsche, and Freud. So if we find ourselves religious and are at all alive to the intellectual climate of the last two centuries, a host of vexing questions immediately assails us. How, for instance, do faith and science go together, or do they? And, as already observed, how can a God of love be responsible for a world such as ours, filled as it is to overflowing with evils beyond reckoning?

George, who grew up in secularized Britain, offers us no apologetics, no reasoned attempt to defend what he says about God. This is certainly not because he did not himself have questions about his faith. Those who knew him well inform us that George read voraciously, and not just Hindu and Eastern literature. Moreover, in an interview granted shortly after George's death, Deepak Chopra, the best-selling author, holistic health guru, and close friend of George in the latter years of his life, was asked, "Did you ever talk to [George] about what he expected or hoped his next life would be?" Chopra's surprising answer to this was, "No, we talked more in trying to figure out scientifically whether there is any validity in the concept [of an afterlife] and how would he explain the survival of consciousness after death."[8] Someone who worried about the problem of the soul in a scientific age must have worried about much else besides. Although George may at one point have heeded Timothy Leary's advice to "turn off your mind, relax, float downstream,"[9] he didn't make that the rule for the rest of his life.

If naïveté is not the explanation for George's total lack of self-defense in controversial religious matters, there are at least two good explanations. One is simply the medium. Music is not an all-purpose vehicle. It can communicate much, but it cannot communicate everything. One can use it effectively to confess one's feelings; one cannot so easily use it to communicate one's rational analysis of any involved issue. We love music because it summons emotions, not because it calls forth thought. Although one may superimpose language upon notes, the sound and the rhythm remain primary. Critical history and quantum physics are accordingly housed in academic journals and books, not in popular music. So too the reasoned defense of religion. It is no mystery that one fails to find reasons for belief or explication of doctrine in Christian hymnals. Songs to and about God are for the heart more than for the mind. They are sung during worship services, which are typically occasions for something other than philosophical reflection. It is the same with Harrisongs: They are first and foremost emotive and evocative. The words always come lashed to the music, and the latter targets our emotions, not our minds.

But it is not just the affecting nature of music that explains the check on George's theological musings. We should also bear in mind that he was not a formally trained academic or intellectual,[10] not even a writer of nonacademic prose. He was a religious individual who experienced God first through the heart and only secondly through his mind. His religion was fundamentally experiential, not cerebral. So instead of engagement with philosophers, his music gives us something more like poetry. As "Far East Man" puts it, George's heart is in charge; he does what it says. In like fashion, "Fish On The Sand" is a complaint about a lack of religious feeling, not a lack of rational conviction. George's songs are in general an expression of what the composer felt, as he clearly says again and again. From first to last they speak of his heart. Personal experience is what counts.

George once wrote: "If there's a God, I want to see Him. It's pointless to believe in something without proof, and Krsna Consciousness and meditation are methods where you can actually obtain GOD perception. You can actually see God, and hear Him, play with Him. It might sound crazy, but He is actually there, actually with you."[11] For the ex-Beatle, knowledge of God comes not from books or ancient authorities or ratiocination but from observable fact—a circumstance that he would have found acknowledged by some of the Hindu thinkers he revered. He read, for example, Radhakrishnan, perhaps the twentieth century's best-known Hindu philosopher. Radhakrishnan was much influenced by liberal Christian theologians who identified true religion with neither doctrine nor ritual but with experience. From this point of view, true religion is insight into the nature of reality and ordering one's life according to that reality, and such insight comes from experience that is self-validating, experience that doesn't require rational argument or even religious tradition.[12]

George's own clear testimony in any case is that God did not beckon to him through argument or tradition. George indeed claimed to have come to God through direct experience mediated by LSD (which he probably took for the first time in early 1965).[13] Looking back from 1987, he said this: "[LSD] just opened the door and I experienced really good things. I mean, I never doubted God after that. Before, I was a cynic. I didn't even say the word God; I thought 'bullshit to all that stuff.' But after that, I knew. It was not even a question of 'Is there possibly a God?' I knew absolutely. It's just that big light that goes off in your head."[14]

It is to George's credit that, if hallucinogens—he took at one time or another hashish, marijuana, peyote, LSD, mescaline, and psilocybin, but never morphine or heroin—were the beginning, they were not the end. Surely warned in part by Lennon's deterioration during his two years of constant drug-taking (1967–68), George distanced himself from Timothy Leary's romantic notion of LSD as a sacramental chemical. Aware both of the possibility of bad trips and of the psychological toll drugs can take, George was wise enough to judge that "if you're really hip you don't get involved with LSD and things like that. You see the potential that it has and the good it can do but you also see that you don't really need it. I needed it the first time I had it. It was a good thing, but it showed me that LSD isn't really the answer to everything. It can help you go from A to B but when you get to B you can see C and you see that to get really high you have to do it straight. There are special ways of getting high without drugs—with yoga, meditation, and all those things."[15] Yet despite this prudent distancing from LSD, it remains an important biographical fact that George thought he stumbled upon God through recreational drug use.

Many questions immediately arise at this point. Why did others who took LSD not come to George's unshakeable faith in God? The music of John Lennon, with whom George shared so many psychedelic trips, sometimes belittles religion and even explicitly denies what mattered most to George, the reality of God. How many who took LSD encountered, or thought that they encountered, God as a result, or did George interpret as God the same something others did not so interpret? A few who took acid ended up joining the Weathermen, not the Hare Krishnas. If, further, as appears, LSD primarily enhances perception and the imagination, should we wager that George's religious impulse was, despite his belief to the contrary, already there before he imbibed, so that drugs only nurtured a seed that had already been planted? We know that George had mystical experiences of some sort as a child,[16] and we also know that he always had affection for his parents, especially his mother, who was a pious Catholic (unlike his father, who was a lapsed Anglican, not religious); so perhaps her religion had a profound and positive impact upon George despite his deep and abiding hostility toward the Roman Catholic Church.

Whatever answers one may return, the pharmacological circumstances of George's conversion tell us that his initial faith was not the upshot of study or argument. Things were no different with his subsequent faith, at least to judge from his music, which values religious experience so highly. George indeed appears to have been a sort of mystic. The premiere piece of evidence for this is in the sadly too-little known, "Sat Singing." The title is a wordplay, which must be lost on most Western listeners. Not only is *Sat* one of the loaded Hindu words for "existence" or "truth," but *satsanga* refers to a religious gathering or service, and one of George's heroes, Paramahansa Yogananda, founded the Yogoda Satsanga Society of India, which in the West became the Self-Realization Fellowship. (George sometimes visited the SRF's Ashram Center in Encinitas, California, when he was in the area.)

Although "Sat Singing" appeared among the songs George initially submitted for *Somewhere In England*, it was not written for the charts (although it's musically satisfying enough), and the profit-driven record executives were not persuaded that it or other songs on the album had a sufficiently popular sound to sell well. The result was that George removed four of the submitted songs and replaced them with others (which in retrospect are inferior to the dumped originals). To my knowledge, one can now find "Sat Singing" (apart from bootlegs) only on the obscure, hard-to-get, and very expensive *Songs By George Harrison*.

"Sat Singing" is, in any event, the musical record of a religious bliss. A reference to the sun at midday and a reference to the sun low on the horizon frame the verbal content. So the experience occupies an entire afternoon. In narrating this intense religious episode, the composer recounts closing his eyes and letting go of all conscious thought, with the result that God comes into his heart. God then speaks, declaring that he is always there, waiting to be loved. God then asks to stay, instructing George to surrender completely. Then the singer begins to come back to mundane reality, as if awakening from a dream. But he remains immersed in a "golden flow" and feels himself "becoming part" of God.

What should we make of this account? Much of what happens to us cannot be put into words, at least adequately, and George certainly shared the common conviction that words fail miserably to communicate mystical encounters.[17] So it might seem pointless to try to recover what happened to him. But when we remember that mystical experiences, according to the testimonies of those who have had them, often involve the perception of a preternatural light, we face an interesting possibility. Not only does "Sat Singing" twice refer to the sun's light, but the singer perceives himself as resting in a "golden flow."

One must wonder whether this is not more than metaphor. In line with this, in "Blow Away," George speaks of closing his eyes and of his head filling with light. My hunch is that, on more than one occasion, George's meditation led him to perceive some sort of extraordinary light. The experience is well attested among contemplatives of all faiths, and the supposition would at least help explain his obsession with light, which he so often associates with the divine. Typical in this connection is one of his last songs, "Rising Sun." Here George instructs listeners that they can perceive in the rising sun their own inner reality. Such reality is—in words that recall one of the songs on The Beatles' *Revolver*—"here and there and nowhere and everywhere." The outer corresponds to the inner. The sun in the sky, which gives all life, represents the divine light of life within.

Another intriguing instance of George's interest in light appears in "Headed For The Light," a song he wrote for The Traveling Wilburys. This is a rather bouncy meditation on the vanities of the present life as compared with the reality of God. Here George reflects on his mistakes and how lost he was at one time. But he now sees the sun ahead and is not ever going to look back. He is heading for the light, which is clearly a synonym for God. To what extent the song looks beyond death is hard to determine. There could well be a glance at the stereotypical Near Death Experience, during which individuals leave their bodies and go down a tunnel, where at the end they encounter a light or a being of light.[18] However that may be, elsewhere, in "Life Itself," George speaks explicitly of "the light in death." He apparently envisages the world to come as a world of light.

While it remains impossible for us to hazard much more than that George probably had mystical experiences featuring light, one aspect of his experience with God can be considered more directly. This is his understanding of God as savior. Often in his music, George, sounding like many Christians, depicts himself as having been lost and then found, as being saved by the grace of God. His music is his personal testimony, his witness that God has changed his life. He belongs, as we shall see in chapter 8, to the company of what the *Bhagavad-Gita* calls the "twiceborn" (1:7).

In "That Which I Have Lost," which manages to combine a country-western feel with strong memories of Johnny Mercer's version of "Accentuate the Positive (Mister In-Between)," George tells us that "all had seemed lost" until a "light" from heaven came to him. He describes this light as a "flash" of "inward illumination" of his consciousness. This illumination removed the darkness from him. It enriched his life more than he can put into words: scales fell from his eyes; it was like life being renewed by the rain, and like the bolts of a prison door opening.

Similar is "Try Some Buy Some," from *Living In The Material World*. Here the singer professes that he had nothing and saw nothing until he called upon God's love, which then came into him. This contrast between before and after, attributed to an encounter with the divine love, comes from the early 1970s and is perhaps close enough to his religious turn in the 1960s that it, like "Long, Long, Long" on *The Beatles (The White Album)*, may be a reflection of some sort of conversion experience. It is then George's version of "Amazing Grace," a retrospect on his initial turn to God.

Other references to a before and an after do not seem, however, to hark back to the mid-1960s, when George found religion. "Headed For The Light," from the years with The Traveling Wilburys, offers a lengthy litany of the singer's woes and his wayward condition. It is as though he were in a confessional, and as though we are his confessor:

* He wandered around with nothing to do.
* He was lost in the night.
* He had no vision of God.
* He suffered depression and loneliness.
* He skirted "the edge" and barely hung on.

- He was rolled in thorns.
- He was unable to see the warning signs.
- He lived under a dark cloud.
- He almost drowned when the rains came.
- He was ignorant of his true condition.
- His shoes were worn out by walking down the same old road.
- His hands were tied.
- He was surrounded by jokers and fools.
- He was in a hole.

Happily, all this weakness, confusion, and misery have given way to a new and better state. George now is, as the title has it, heading for the light. He has flown away from his self-deprecating catalog, with its sins and traps and bewilderment. He sees the sun ahead and, unlike Lot's wife in the famous biblical story, he is never going to look back. Nothing can stop him as his dreams are coming true while he ruminates upon God.

My own inclination is to interpret this song, not as an account, twenty-five years or so after the event, of a dramatic conversion, but instead as notice of the end of the period of emptiness reflected in *Cloud Nine*'s "Fish On The Sand," or a subsequent period analogous to it. George's passion for God was just that, a passion, and all passions wax and wane. In this, George was no different than the rest of us. He must have felt more religious and have put more energy into his devotional activities at some times than at others. *Cloud Nine* documents a down time, "Headed For The Light" an up time.

In this connection it is interesting to speculate about "Rising Sun," one of George's last songs. Here he goes on at length about how sick he was before God sent to him a "messenger from inner space," a signal he had long disregarded. One could understand this as an interpretation of George's early, LSD-induced Damascus Road experience, his committing of himself to God in the 1960s: He was lost, but then he was found. Yet it is more likely, given the late date of "Rising Sun," that the lyrics refer to some experience toward the end of his life, when he rededicated his life to God. He had, according to his own perception, fallen away; now he's back.

Conjecturing further, I am inclined to believe that this song may well give us George's ruminations after his close encounter with death at the hand of a crazed fan in 1999. This frightening event, it appears, prodded him to realize that he was not as prepared for leaving life as he may have thought. Although his wife tells us that he yelled out "Hare Krishna" during the attack, there is evidence that being stabbed and believing he would die increased his felt need for God and so revealed his prior condition to be deficient. The opening line of "Looking For My Life," also from *Brainwashed*, strongly hints at this. Here George addresses the Lord and confesses that he must find his way back. I take these words to be an admission that, when death came, George found he was not wholly ready, found that he was not religiously where he wanted to be. He had not sufficiently practiced the art of dying.

"Stuck Inside A Cloud," another track from *Brainwashed*, narrates some sort of crisis, perhaps at or about the same time. The song speaks of not getting enough sleep, smoking too much, losing concentration, crying, being alone, not wanting to eat, and feeling crazy. Such anxiety and sadness seem due to the realization that nothing matters except touching "your lotus feet," which is a Hindu idiom for a student's devotion to a teacher or God.[19] The longing to be back where he belongs is patent. Again one infers that, in George's mind, he has somehow retreated from his earlier commitment to God, or at least not moved on to where he should be.

My own sense from the entirety of George's musical corpus is that, while there is an initial conversion experience, there is, especially after the release of *Living In The Material World*, and so after the early years of religious zeal, a recurring oscillation, a regular slackening of devotional commitment followed by a renewed resolution to put God first. George's dramatic conversion was trailed by times of greater and lesser enthusiasm, and so he found himself amending his ways and surrendering to God over and over.

It accords with this reading that, throughout the Harrison corpus, God remains an object of longing. Bliss never lasts. The divine presence comes and goes. Problems always return. Such inevitable vacillation may even begin to some degree with "My Sweet Lord," in which George offers that he really wants to see and to be with God—as though, in some important sense, he hasn't yet seen or already been with God. Similarly, in "Give Me Love," from *Living In The Material World*, George fervently tries to reach God with his heart and with his soul, which implies some present deficiency. So there is an ongoing search. In the achingly beautiful, "The Light That Has Lighted The World," the singer confesses that he is still trying to perceive that supernatural light. George nowhere claims to have arrived; he is rather always a pilgrim, always on the road. In the words of "The Day The World Gets 'Round," he is one of those who has "made a start," nothing more. Like the rest of us, he is always beginning again.

Notes

1. George's solo career actually began when he was still with The Beatles. In 1968, he produced both *Wonderwall*, the instrumental soundtrack for a film of the same name, and *Electronic Sound*, an avant-garde experiment, which sadly lives up to its title: it's sound, not music.

2. George Harrison, *I, Me, Mine* (San Francisco: Chronicle Books, 2002), 274. His brief commentary on the song ends with this: "It's about a dishonest Red Indian Chief [JOKE]." This obviously reflects his reticence to say it is about suicide. But he once said that "you either go crackers and commit suicide or you try to realize something and attach yourself more strongly to an inner strength" (Alan Clayson, *George Harrision* [rev. ed.; London: Sanctuary, 2001], 341). This is autobiographical.

3. *Melody Maker*, September 6, 1975. He also said of this time: "I was in a real down place."

4. See esp. George's preface to the two-volume work, *Krsna: The Supreme Personality of Godhead. A Summary Study of Śrīa Vyāsadeva's Śrīmad-Bhāgavatam, Tenth Canton* (New York: Bhaktivedanta Book Trust, 1970), by A. C. Bhaktivedanta Swami Prabhupāda, founder of the International Society for Krishna Consciousness.

5. Interview by Mukunda Goswami, available online at: www.krishna.org/Articles/2000/08/00066.html.

6. Interview in *Crawdaddy*, February, 1977. There is an online version, available at: www.geocities.com/~beatleboy1/dbgh277.int.html.

7. The concert was reissued on a CD in 2005 along with a documentary that includes some previously unseen performances.

8. The whole interview is available online at: www.beliefnet.com/story/94/story_9434.html.

9. Timothy Leary, Ralph Metzner, and Richard Alpert, *The Psychedelic Experience: A Manual Based on the Tibetan Book of the Dead* (New Hide Park, NY: University Books, 1964), 14. Lennon quoted this line in The Beatles' "Tomorrow Never Knows."

10. He in fact once commented that intellectuals "will always have problems, because they always need to 'know.' They're often the most spiritually bankrupt people, because they never let go; they don't understand the meaning of 'to transcend' the intellect. But an ordinary person's more willing to say, 'Okay, let me try it and see if it works" (1982 interview by Mukunda Goswami, available online at: www.krishna.org/Articles/2000/08/00066.html).

11. Preface to *Krsna*.

12. S. Radhakrishnan, *The Hindu View of Life* (London: George Allen & Unwin, 1927), 15.

13. George may not, at first, have interpreted his LSD experiences as encounters with God, for The Byrds' Roger McGuinn has said that, when he asked Harrison, in the summer of 1965, whether he believed in God, he got this answer: "Well, we [The Beatles—the plural is fascinating] don't know about that yet." See Denny Somach, Kathleen Somach, and Kevin Gunn, *Ticket to Ride* (New York: William Morrow & Co., 1989), 212.

14. Interview in *Creem*, December 1987, January 1988. A similar statement appears in Harrision, *I, Me, Mine*, 44–45: "Out of the LSD madness (and there were a few horrors) there came a few 'zaps.' It made me laugh. I'd never thought about, couldn't even say the word 'God.' It embarrassed me, but you know it was so strange, GOD, and it washed away all these fears and doubts and little things that hang you up."

15. Derek Taylor, *It Was Twenty Years Ago Today* (New York: Simon & Schuster, Inc., 1987), 126–27.

16. For George's own words on the subject see the February 1977 *Crawdaddy* interview, online at: www.geocities.com/~beatleboy1/dbgh277.int.html.

17. Cf. Harrison, *I, Me, Mine*, 45: "Sometimes you just want to yell about God because it's right there, but the moment you try and explain it, it's like rabbiting."

18. It might also reflect, if the story is true, a vision of Harry Harrison, George's father, on the day of Harry's death: George reportedly saw him appear in a blue and gold light and bid him and his brothers good-bye. See Geoffrey Giuliano, *Dark Horse: The Private Life of George Harrison* (New York: Dutton, 1990), 162.

19. In the previous line he recounts that "he made an exhibition." This is probably a reference to his trip to Australia in 1982 to help launch his friend Derek Taylor's book, *Fifty Years Adrift*.

Use My Body Like a Car

HUMAN NATURE

*M*ost people, in most times and places, have been dualists. They have believed that the human being consists not just of a body but also of a soul or spirit, some nonmaterial portion or aspect of the self that is capable of surviving physical death. The far-flung inclination to perceive ourselves in these terms has, however, encountered strong opposition in recent decades. We can no longer assume its truth as a matter of course. Since the rise and success of the modern mechanistic sciences, and perhaps especially since the advent of the neurosciences, many have found it harder and harder to imagine that there is any element of human nature that is not, in the final analysis, material, or dependent upon material processes. Can we be anything more than complex chemical and electrical machines that have, by some trick still not understood, generated the magical thing we call "consciousness"? And when our machines cease to function, doesn't self-awareness dissipate and, whether we like it or not, go away forever?

George, whatever his knowledge of the modern scientific and philosophical debates about this issue, emphatically did not think so. Faithfully and without apology representing popular Hindu tradition, his songs at many points presuppose a robust, old-fashioned dualism. In his music, the true self indeed already exists before it is born into the material world. The self then experiences physical existence by way of a body, which is its vehicle or instrument. Finally, when that body wears out or becomes too damaged, the true self exits, either to enter some better realm of existence, or to come back into another body for another round in the material world. As it says in the *Bhagavad-Gita*: "Just as a person casts off worn-out garments and puts on others that are new, even so does the embodied soul cast off worn-out bodies and take on others that are new" (2:22).

A dualistic anthropology was not, for George, of marginal importance. It was rather central to his self-conception and worldview. He once in fact said that he was not "George," by which he meant this: "I am this living thing that goes on, always has been, always will be, but at this time I happen to be in 'this' body. The body has changed; [it] was a baby, was a young man, will soon be an old man, and I'll be dead. The physical body will pass but this bit in the middle, that's the only reality."[1] In line with this, "Living In The Material World" speaks of the self using its body just as a driver uses a car, to get from here to there. "George" is not the machine that is his body.

George's dualism, far from being just a theoretical or intellectual conviction, was, as we can see from his music, faithful to his experience: he sensed a strong disjunction between the inward and the outward. "Pisces Fish," from late in his career, offers a telling illustration. This lovely song opens by dispassionately gathering disparate images from ordinary life—rowers on a river, geese on a riverbank, a broken-down bicycle, old ladies walking and training their dogs, a farmer complaining about the personal cost of mad cow disease. George's response to this catalogue of the mundane is unexpected because it is seemingly unrelated: "I'm a Pisces fish and the river runs through my soul." We have here the disjunction of two realities. On the one hand is external reality, everything going on in the world of the five senses, captured in

George's list of run-of-the-mill scenes. On the other hand is the far more important inner reality, the divine river of life that runs through George's soul. The one, compared to the other, is uninteresting, even inconsequential. The inner trumps the outer, resulting in a sort of metaphysical alienation.

This emphasis upon the disparity between the outer and the inner, with preference going to the latter, derives partly from Hinduism and especially from the philosophy of the *Bhagavad-Gita*, where pleasure and pain, gain and loss, victory and defeat—that is, all of our experiences in the body—are ultimately of like consequence, which means of no consequence, for they all pass away and are forgotten. Earthly circumstances are only for a season. The vital, eternal reality lies elsewhere, in the self that transcends temporal existence. So the true sage, at the end of the day, has no interest in "the actions that he has done" or in "the actions that he has not done" (*Bhagavad-Gita* 3:18). The eternal yanks the attention of the wise away from the temporal, for what matters is not the fleeting body and its material enclosure but the everlasting soul and the eternal Reality behind or beyond all mundane reality. This is why George can sing, in "I Live For You," that, regarding this world, he hasn't a care.

George's relative indifference to or even estrangement from the world at large was also an inheritance from his days with The Beatles and their self-indulgent experiences with hard drugs. Discovery of and exploration of the inner world of the mind can render routine life in the so-called real world relatively uninteresting. Lennon's LSD-inspired "I'm Only Sleeping" on *Revolver* is, for instance, about disinterestedly observing the world speeding by outside his window while the important things take place within the tranquil singer, who pleads to be left alone, so that he can "float upstream" and mentally see the sights on display in the antipode of his mind.

At about the same time, George himself was writing the sitar-based "The Inner Light." This hymn to quietism, originally the B-side single for "Lady Madonna" and later an entry on The Beatles' *Past Masters, Vol. 2*, was composed during the *Magical Mystery Tour* sessions (1968). It is a remarkable statement of the independent vitality of the inner life. The words, taken from the *Tao Te Ching*, which was so popular with the counterculture in the late 1960s, relativize and even disparage knowledge of the external world.² One can know "all things of earth" without walking out one's front door, and one can know "the ways of heaven" without gazing through one's window. Indeed, attention to the world at large can be a distraction: the more physical travel, the less real knowledge. One reaches the most important destination not by moving about or by looking or doing but rather by seeking for what the title calls "The Inner Light." Implicit is the darkness of the external world, a theme repeated in many of George's later solo records.

Although the words of "The Inner Light" are from the *Tao Te Ching*, they faithfully convey George's lasting outlook. His lyrics, over the entire course of his career, exhibit a strong tendency to see the world from a distance, to think of it as being "out there," and of much less interest than what is "in here," his own inscape. This is perhaps one reason why his songs are almost devoid of geography, why they are so little interested in the places George has been. Unlike the music Ray Davies wrote for The Kinks, which is so rich in references to English locales, especially London locales—so much so that there are Internet sites with the relevant maps and pictures—Harrisongs generally neglect their concrete, earthly settings. There are no nostalgic musings about "Strawberry Fields" or "Penny Lane." One of George's albums is appropriately entitled *Somewhere In England*: exactly where doesn't matter. Similarly, on "Woman Don't You Cry For Me," George says, "There's no one place I want to be."

Reversing modern materialistic prejudice, which bestows reality upon matter while remaining unsure what to make of consciousness, George views the external, material world as a subjective dream, his own inner self as the authentic reality. Observing the outside world with authentic detachment, he is not really part of what passes before his eyes. This is so much a part of George's experience that, in "Pisces Fish," his life feels "like fiction." In other words, his days in this material world have been somehow unreal, like a shadow, and he longs for fuller experience of a nonmaterial world. He is just passing through on his way to something better. It is telling that, after George died, his family released a statement which equated his passing with "awakening from this dream."

George's dualism and earthly disaffection make death a welcome eventuality, as we shall see in a later chapter. Death is not a curse but a blessing. It is the inevitable splitting of the union of the inner and the outer, a rupture that those properly prepared happily anticipate. Death is escape from the limitations of the cage of matter in which we are now imprisoned. If one has not lived wisely, of course, one may be reincarnated, be drawn back into another body for another lifetime. The goal, however, is to avoid the transmigratory cycle of births and deaths and so to move on to a higher reality. That, indeed, is salvation, to get back out of this material world. Our true citizenship lies elsewhere.

One guesses that George's confident belief in a nonmaterial self was partly fuelled by his drug consumption. Not only can LSD make one feel detached from the world as we normally perceive it and reveal that the "real world" of everyday perception is not the only world, but it can also stimulate out-of-body experiences, during which one's consciousness seems to separate from one's physical frame. Sometimes people even view their bodies from afar. George took enough drugs that he almost certainly knew firsthand what this is like; and it would be altogether natural to construe an out-of-body experience, taken at face value, as a sort of foretaste of or rehearsal for death, when the soul will leave the body for good.

As already indicated, George's dualism is not morally neutral. In a way reminiscent of Plato and Christian ascetics, it is not just that the inner and the outer are two metaphysically different sorts of things: it is that the one counts so much more than the other. Indeed, whereas proper attention to the soul wins salvation, attachment to the physical, external world leaves the soul unattached to God. While George never disparages the body as evil, he does in one place belittle it as "a bag of bones."[3] He clearly relegates it to secondary importance.

While only occasionally assuring us that God is in the sun and moon and other people, what George tells us again and again is that the Eternal dwells within the self. Like the Christian mystic William Law, he seems to have believed that "though God is everywhere present, yet He is only present to thee in the deepest and most central part of thy soul." So the "big message," in George's view of things, is to "look for the light," and that means undertaking an inward journey.[4] Salvation results from self-discovery. As "Love Comes To Everyone" has it, inside one's heart is the divine love and reality "that's never changing . . . never aging." Finding that love is the one thing needful.

Even if we don't know it, then, we carry around inside ourselves the answers to life's supreme riddles. As "Within You Without You" has it, "It's all within yourself." Although that song comes from the 1960s, George thought in these terms to the end, as is manifest in "Any Road" on *Brainwashed*. Here the truth is "so far out" that "the way out is in." He is telling us that, although people may be incredulous ("so far out"), the solution to the human predicament lies not outside the self but rather within, because that is where the sacred living water flows and we can encounter the Deity. Within the human heart is a divine inscription that, when unconcealed, conquers our ignorance.

George says this straight out in the lively "Crackerbox Palace," the bizarre video for which is now available on the DVD in the 2004 anthology, *The Dark Horse Years 1976–1992*. The song declares simply, "the Lord is well and inside of you." On one level, this is a reference to the offbeat comedian, Lord Buckley, whose recordings George, like Bob Dylan, much admired in the sixties.[5] But George was fond of the double entendre, and "Crackerbox Palace" is clearly a sort of allegory in which the palace represents the world. And God, a bit like the memory and inspiration of Lord Buckley, resides within. This is why we can, to recall "Awaiting On You All," do just fine without church house and temple. The kingdom of heaven is within. As it says in the *Bhagavad-Gita*, "He who finds his happiness within, his joy within, and likewise his light only within, that yogin becomes divine and attains to the beatitude of God" (5:24).

How does George perceive the relationship of his individual soul to the universal Deity? There is an affinity and even, from one point of view, identity between the two. If God is eternal, so is the soul, as the liner notes to *Brainwashed* make explicit: "'There never was a time when you or I did not exist. Nor will there be any future when we shall cease to be' (Krishna to Arjuna in the *Bhagavad-Gita*)." These words, echoed in "Any Road," are from *Bhagavad-Gita* 2:20: "He is never born, nor does he die at any time, nor having once come to be does he again cease to be. He is unborn, eternal, permanent, and primeval. He is not slain when the body is slain" (2:20). Here the true human self is identified with the Eternal, and George elsewhere reckons "eternity" to be one of the chief characteristics of the Deity (for example, in "Brainwashed"). In this and other respects, George endorses the doctrine of the Hare Krishnas, who taught him that just "as a single drop of water has the same qualities as an ocean of water, so has our consciousness the qualities of God's consciousness."[6] George did insist that "none of us are God—just His servants,"[7] but he also said, in a press conference in 1974 in Los Angeles, "From the Hindu point of view each soul is potentially divine, [and] the goal is to manifest the divinity.... Every one of us has within us a drop of that ocean and we have the same qualities as God, just like a drop of the ocean has the same qualities as the whole ocean. Everybody's looking for something and we are it. We don't have to look anywhere—it's right there within ourselves."

One of the more arresting descriptions of the correlation between the divine Self and the human self occurs on "Rising Sun." Here the singer gazes at the heavenly sun as it comes up over the horizon. He not only feels its warmth but also understands that he is somehow at one with the orb in the sky. There is, moreover, a sun not only before his eyes without but also a sun within, present to his mind's eye. George, here at his poetic best, confesses that he, like the sun, is a billion years old, and also that, just as the sun gives life, so does the light within himself. This is why he can observe that the rising sun, which here stands for God, is actually "inside of you."

The participation of the soul in the supreme divine nature is probably yet one more aspect of George's theology that, although it comes from Hinduism, can also perhaps be related to his experience with hallucinogens. Depersonalization, or a loss of ego, is, as Aldous Huxley famously found out on his first try,[8] a common response to the ingestion of mescalin, LSD, and kindred drugs. The drug culture, instructed by Timothy Leary and his like, thought this a good thing and appealed for support to the mystical traditions of the world. Leary and his adherents harked back to the experiences of Meister Eckhart and other mystics in both East and West, mystics who, while confessing their experiences ineffable, nonetheless spoke of a state in which they felt at one with the universe.

Now George, in his drug-taking days, must have felt some degree of depersonalization, and perhaps even a sense of oneness with the universe. The experience is real enough (and can come out of nowhere even without drugs, as I know from one afternoon in my own life many years ago). Such firsthand experience, which could also have come to

George, as it has to others, through Transcendental Meditation, would certainly have added plausibility not only to his Hindu ideas about how illusory our perception of the world can be, but also plausibility to the proposal that human nature is part and parcel of the universal reality behind all existence. The Supreme Nature, being not only above all but also in all, is necessarily within each of us.

A sense of depersonalization lies behind George's comments about his self or ego not really existing. His wife Olivia (whom he met on his 1974 American tour) recounted that "George was always quick to point out that in reality there is no I, Me or Mine."[9] When he entitled his reminiscences, *I, Me, Mine*, after one of his contributions to The Beatles' *Let It Be*, he intended it as irony. This is why, in "I Live For You," he can say that, in this world, he doesn't own a thing. Despite his success and wealth, or perhaps it would be better to say because of it, he has come to realize that what is important doesn't lie in the material world. He accordingly attempts to slay his craving ego and cultivate a holy indifference, trying to be, in the words of the *Gita*, "devoid of any sense of mineness or egotism" (2:71). George wanted to rid himself of "I, Me, Mine." Maybe this is what he means when he sings, at the end of "Only A Northern Song," that "there's no one there."

George's dualistic anthropology, his estrangement from the world, and his religious focus don't comport well with widespread contemporary convictions and attitudes—a circumstance that, incidentally, explains some of the undeserved antagonism in reviews of his music. It is far from obvious to many modern people that the material world is not our home, and equally not evident to many that we are in our innermost selves an indestructible piece of the divine reality. George's theology is quite remote from many. He, however, was comfortable with the notion that ordinary perception is deceptive, and that most people have everything upside down and just can't see the truth of things.

The music of The Beatles already pays a great deal of attention to the problems of perception. Songs such as "Rain," "Tomorrow Never Knows," "And Your Bird Can Sing," and "A Day In The Life" are all about this topic; and they perhaps hint at something akin to William Blake's famous remark, taken up by Aldous Huxley, that the doors of perception need to be cleansed: the eyes in the head don't reveal all that there is. George himself, in any case, could confidently assert, "most people's reality is an illusion, a great big illusion."[10] By this he did not mean that we sometimes fool ourselves about this or that. He meant instead that the majority of human beings are the victims of a fundamental misperception. Seeing may be believing, but it may likewise be misleading. Deceived by their everyday senses, many fail to grasp the true nature of the creation and of themselves. They live in a profound ignorance, misled by misplaced desire; they wander adrift through thoughtless identification with and attachment to the material world.

In the catchy "Awaiting On You All," from *All Things Must Pass*, George uses the language of pollution to describe this sad state of acute illusion in which so many carelessly spend their lives. He likewise adopts traditional Christian language to say the same thing in a different way, characterizing his listeners as "fallen." Whatever the metaphor for our illness, we get well by becoming awake, by opening our spiritual eyes so that we "see" reality as it is. Also on *All Things Must Pass*, in the "Art Of Dying," George preaches, while Eric Clapton's guitar wails in the background, that maybe the approach of death will reveal that the "things that seemed so very plain" will show themselves to be painful lies. Maybe, but maybe only when it is too late, will one see that one has lived a lie, been entrapped in a grand chimera of the brain.

Perhaps the finest expression of everyday perception as ultimately illusory appears on *All Things Must Pass*'s "Beware Of Darkness." Here George warns all of us to watch out and take care. The reason? The earnest singer perceives the human individual to be an "unconscious sufferer" who wanders aimlessly. People may be awake, but they are still asleep, their eyes closed. They know neither where they have come from nor where they are going, nor why they suffer as they do. The song sums up its warning with the words, "Beware of Mâya." This admonition takes up the Indian concept of illusion or appearance, found already in the old Hindu texts known as the *Upanishads*. To comprehend *mâya* is to reject consensus reality, to regard it as merely a mental construction, a collective dream of our multiple minds— impermanent and subject to change. Authentic reality, God's reality, is something beyond, something we can't see with our bodily eyes, something other than what everybody else seems to agree upon. While the gate of true perception is narrow, and those who find it are few, those passing through the wide gate of the world's amalgamated reality are many. Blinded by desire, the latter are, as "The Day The World Gets 'Round" harshly puts it, full of "foolishness."

The paradox here is on full display in a cartoonish drawing from George himself that concludes the liner notes to *Brainwashed*. To the left we see a collection of crude, crowded, tall buildings. They clearly represent the typical metropolis, a place where human beings congregate in large numbers. To the right, and significantly apart from the urban sketch, is a serene, disembodied head. Its hair is long and its eyes are closed. It chants, as the bubble caption informs us, "God—God—God." At the bottom, in parenthesis, is a famous line from the Bible, from the prophet Isaiah and the Gospels, "A voice cry's [*sic*] in the Wilderness."[11] Above this caption is a sign that, pointing to the crowded city, declares simply, "Bullshit Avenue."

The meaning of the images is transparent. The head is George engaged in chanting, and the moral of the whole picture is that it is he, the man with his eyes closed, seeking God, who truly sees. Those who fill the city and walk along Bullshit Avenue dwell in a wilderness; and while their eyes may be open, they are in truth sightless. In the language of "All Those Years Ago," not many have ears, for attuned to the noise of the city, its citizens are deaf to the wisdom of the religious message that George, as a latter-day prophet, faithfully chants. The man who looks unconscious is the conscious one. The masses in the city, who seem to be awake, are actually asleep.

This severe, condescending assessment of the disoriented human crowd—an assessment which, in its simplicity, is unfair to the masses because it underestimates the depth and struggles of ordinary people—has its musical counterpart in "Unconsciousness Rules." This jaunty tune, which first of all mocks those who pass their evenings partying in the discothèques (and which reflects George's distaste for seventies disco music), has a serious side to it. Those who foolishly fill their empty lives with dances and parties—as George himself had once done—typify the human condition: we all preoccupy ourselves with dead-end distractions. Sounding a bit like the dour Catholic apologist, Blaise Pascal, George mourns that we tend to heed our irrational impulse to seek divertissement, preferring easy and empty activities to the arduous but infinitely more important and more rewarding task of seeking God. We become so caught up in so many idiotic activities that the "unconsciousness rules," that is, our unenlightened minds command our lives. Society itself cheers us on, for it reinforces our faulty instincts by telling us, in the words of "Crackerbox Palace," to "do what the rest all do." The collectivity commends its illusion to the individual. We are not only blind in ourselves, but so is the larger social body. The blind lead the blind—a biblical image George borrows and inserts toward the end of "Unconsciousness Rules."

That the world at large is an illusion, and that most people pass their lives without understanding this poignant fact or living in its light, make human existence an overwhelming tragedy. We do not know that our apparent freedoms are ultimately illusory and that we are actually like animals trapped in a zoo—our cages being self-constructed out of ignorance. This sad circumstance is the chief force behind the recurrent gloom and preoccupation with misfortune in George's music. His guitar "gently weeps" because so many of the souls embodied in the material world are "diverted," "perverted," and "inverted." When George asks, "Isn't It A Pity?," the scope of his question is vast: it embraces almost everything.

"I Live For You" records George's bereavement over the pitiable state of our hoodwinked world. In this, with his slide guitar sounding particularly doleful, and a country twang further enhancing the melancholy, the singer depicts himself as alone, cheerless, and full of sorrow. Light has been banished, so he dwells in darkness, weeping many tears, hoping that he can somehow feel God's presence within him. He suffers in this miserable state because he lives in an overwhelmingly "sad world," as another song, "Who Can See It," puts it. Acutely cognizant that people in general are blithely unaware of their true nature, are alienated from the divine light within, and are fated to return to this material world with its overabundance of ills, how can George not feel burdened by a "heavy load" ("Give Me Love"), by "the hopelessness" around him ("Beware Of Darkness")? "Far East Man" even goes so far as to describe life on earth as "hellish."

When trying to understand the depth of George's melancholy and even cynicism, it is perhaps not enough to consider his adherence to the sober Hindu concept of *māya* and his enthusiastic initiation into hallucinogens. We should also take due account of his often shy and inwardly focused personality. It takes little imagination to see how easily a philosophical Hinduism, with its emphasis upon detachment and the inner realm, might appeal to one who often found life in the material world unfulfilling and empty, and who could experience large numbers of people as a burden rather than a delight.

In many respects George was, in the terminology of Jung, an introvert. Despite his good humor, his many friends, and his ability to play the role of public performer, he tended to be firstly concerned with and interested in his own mental and spiritual life. Leaving aside the little known instrumental, "Cry For A Shadow" (1961), his first song was, fittingly, "Don't Bother Me" (August 1963). Written while he was sick and wanted to be left alone, he asks others not to come around, to stay away. The course of the rest of his life shows that this wish was not just a response to an exceptional occasion, to either illness or a departed girlfriend. George regularly wanted to be alone. After The Beatles broke up, he spent most of his time closed up in his Friar Park mansion and its grounds, gardening, playing his music, and otherwise occupying himself with family, close friends, and God. He was the first Beatle to wear out on the road, declaring after the U.S. tour in 1965 that he wanted to quit the band. He found the world "out there" wearying.

George's introversion is documented on film. The video footage of *The Concert For Bangladesh* reveals a man not wholly comfortable with center stage. In accord with this, George toured very little. It is telling that, on the CD *Live In Japan*, we hear him say at the end: "I'd like to thank the band and Eric [Clapton] for making me come here to Japan." This 1991 tour, George's first since the ill-fated Dark Horse tour of 1974, was not his idea, and it was short-lived.[12]

When one watches the footage from Japan, it is obvious that George is no Paul. Before an audience, Paul McCartney always comes to life, basking in the applause. He draws energy from the enthusiastic crowds. He has toured recurrently since the 1970s because he loves it. George is another story. In the video of his performance in Japan, the front man is a bit ill at ease, not altogether sure of himself. Although George doesn't look unhappy, at the same time the crowd doesn't seem to energize him much. He appears rather to be playing firstly to himself and to his band. His acknowledgments of the audience are brief, and his closing "I love you" strikes one as perfunctory. George was no showman. One has trouble imagining him playing the Super Bowl, as his ex-bandmate Paul has twice.

Although, like a tortoise that pulls its limbs into its shell, George often withdrew, both physically and mentally, from the world at large, he was not, as we shall see below, without a social conscience. Fairness also dictates recognizing that George was not an unbounded cynic, little more than a curmudgeon, like H. L. Mencken, who enjoyed railing at the frightful human circus. His somberness was to some extent balanced by an ability to laugh. He had an obsessive and abiding love for Monty Python, and members of the troupe performed in his memory at *The Concert for George*. He became good friends with Pythoner Eric Idle, and before his shows on the 1974 American tour, George played the Monty Python TV theme song. He was also a big fan of the coarse stand-up comedian Lenny Bruce as well as a friend of brilliant funnyman Peter Sellers, most famed as star of the Pink Panther films. He further much appreciated *The Rutles*, a delightful and rollicking mockumentary of a fictional rock band transparently modeled after The Beatles. Clearly he could laugh heartily even at himself and his famous past. In the statements they issued to the press immediately after George's death, Ringo spoke of George's "sense of laughter," and both Paul McCartney and Michael Palin observed that he cracked jokes until the end.

George's healthy sense of humor is, admittedly, not often on display in his music. It is not, however, altogether absent. In *Cloud Nine*'s upbeat rocker, "Wreck Of The Hesperus," the singer has a good time mocking himself as he tries to make a pop record in middle age (he was then in his forties). He's feeling a bit like Methuselah, and he's no longer a "spring chicken." But though he's "been plucked," he's "still kicking." No less amusing is "This Song," from 1976's *Thirty-Three & 1/3*. Its occasion was the lawsuit—begun in the 1970s and not finished until the 1990s—regarding the inspiration of "My Sweet Lord." The suit accused George of subconsciously plagiarizing "He's So Fine," composed by Ronald Mack in 1962 and performed by the Chiffons in 1963. Setting aside the anger displayed in the earlier "Sue Me, Sue You Blues," which was a response to litigation involving The Beatles, "This Song" prefers to play for laughs. This buoyant example of pop-rock, which made it to number fifteen on the American Billboard chart, happily skewers itself, proclaiming that it is not tricky, doesn't infringe upon anyone's copyright, is neither bad nor good, and has a riff that won't win gold medals. The accompanying video, which is raucous, juvenile, chaotic, and absurdist, and which at the end features George playing his guitar while handcuffed to a guard, mocks the justice of the courtroom.

If George's admitted gloomy side is not without its cheerful twin, if the dark, brooding images on the original "All Things Must Pass" do not cancel the smiling, happy George on the front of *Cloud Nine*, how do the two fit together? How does his humor comport with his cynicism, with his skeptical view of the tragic state of the world? Does his humor cohere with the rest of his thought and music, or is it an unexplained and unassimilated quirk, an eccentric boulder on an otherwise bleak religious landscape? Does George laugh because the hopeless around him would otherwise drive him mad? Is he like medical examiners and coroners who, when confronted with bodily realities that nauseate them, cope with black humor?

My own suggestion is that George's humor is not empty precisely because of his religious faith. His world is not, after all, a Kafkaesque universe in which life has no meaning, in which jokes are just more divertissement. Although at one time he much enjoyed the legendary British TV series, "The Prisoner," in which irrationality rules and no one has answers, he came to believe in a universe pervaded by profound sense and meaning. And despite all the world's darkness and the omnipresence of *mâya*, of illusion, he thought salvation, by God's grace, possible, and indeed believed that salvation would eventually come to everyone. While there is not much collective eschatology in his music, little reflection upon the Hindu cycles of cosmic dissolution and recreation, and certainly nothing comparable to Bob Dylan's "Slow Train Coming," which cryptically announces the second coming of Jesus, George's worldview entails a happy ending, entails what he calls, on *Living In The Material World*, "The Day The World Gets 'Round." Given that we are all at one with the Divinity, and given that God-realization is our birthright, sooner or later we all must come to realize who we are and so obtain *moksha*, liberation. This is what "I'll Still Love You (When Every Song Is Sung)"—written during the sessions for *All Things Must Pass* but given to Ringo for his 1976 album, *Ringo's*

Rotogravure—looks forward to: the time when all souls are "free," when all eyes will "see," and when all human beings will be of the same mind. "All Things Must Pass," but no one really ever passes away.

It is likely enough that such optimism explains what George means when he affirms on his 1979 self-titled album that it's just a matter of time before "love comes to everyone." The subject is, transparently, not human love but divine love. So it seems that all will be well. When he sings, in both "Here Comes The Sun" and "Wreck Of The Hesperus," that "it's alright," I think he means that ultimately everything *is* alright. His optimism is akin to the famous remark of Julian of Norwich, that "all shall be well, and all shall be well, and all manner of thing shall be well." It is such knowledge that not only makes the human tragedy bearable but also gives one leave, in the midst of all the tears, to laugh.

Notes

1. George Harrison, *I, Me, Mine* (San Francisco: Chronicle Books, 2002), 44.
2. George relates, in *I, Me, Mine*, 118, that after he spoke of the Maharishi Mahesh Yogi on *The David Frost Show*, a Cambridge Sanskrit scholar, Juan Mascaró, sent him a copy of one of his books, entitled, *Lamps of Fire from the Scriptures and Wisdom of the World* (London: Methuen, 1961), and called his attention to its translation of *Tao Te Ching* 48 (106–7):

> Without going out of my door
> I can know all things on earth.
> Without looking out of my window
> I can know the ways of heaven.

> For the farther one travels
> The less one knows.

> The sage therefore
> Arrives without traveling
> Sees all without looking,
> Does all without doing.

With only minor changes, these are the lyrics of "The Inner Light."

3. George's preface to A. C. Bhaktivedanta Swami Prabhupāda, *Krsna: The Supreme Personality of Godhead. A Summary Study of Śrīa Vyāsadeva's Śrīmad-Bhāgavatam, Tenth Canton* (New York: Bhaktivedanta Book Trust, 1970).

4. Harrision, *I, Me, Mine*, 44.

5. See Harrison, *I, Me, Mine*, 334.

6. Again I quote George's preface to *Krsna*.

7. Taken from a 1982 interview by Mukunda Goswami, available online at: www.krishna.org/Articles/2000/08/00066.html.

8. Aldous Huxley, *The Doors of Perception* (New York: Harper, 1954).

9. Preface to Harrison, *I, Me, Mine*, 1.

10. Harrison, *I, Me, Mine*, 44.

11. I assume that "cry's" instead of "cries" is a simple mistake, not an intentional alteration full of meaning. One may compare the mistake in the CD booklet to *Thirty Three & 1/3*, where we find "Mr. Grief" in the lyrics of "Crackerbox Palace." But it should be "Mr. Greif," as in the liner notes to the original album; see Harrison, *I, Me, Mine*, 334, 337.

12. George did, nonetheless, publicly say that he enjoyed the experience; he even raised the possibility of touring more, although he never did; see Paul Cashmere's interview of George for *Undercover*, available online at: http://abbeyrd.best.vwh.net/harrison.htm.

Chanting the Name of the Lord

ESTABLISHED RELIGIONS

As a child, George attended Roman Catholic mass with his mother. (His father stayed away.) By the time he was eleven or twelve, he decided it was not for him, and he quit going. He didn't, however, leave without looking back; and when he did so, he didn't like what he saw. He didn't like a faith that seemingly confined itself to weekends. He didn't like kneeling on hard wooden benches. And he didn't like the ecclesiastical artwork—although, at least according to later reminiscence, he was intrigued by the paintings of the Stations of the Cross, which depicted a tortured man dragging a heavy wooden cross. On the whole, George's experience in church was empty, without meaning. The word "religion" ever after seemed to him to refer to something in which he had no interest.

George's overriding response to his childhood Catholicism was not indifference but hostility, and his musical corpus contains more than a trace of anti-Catholicism. The most blatant illustration is "P. 2. Vatican Blues (Last Saturday Night)," on the posthumous *Brainwashed*. Although recorded during the sessions for *Cloud Nine*, the song, for whatever reason, didn't make it to that album.

Despite the humor and the buoyant slide guitar, bitterness and disillusionment animate the song. "P. 2. Vatican Blues (Last Saturday Night)" opens with George happily recalling a recent visit to the Vatican, during which he took delight in gazing at the magnificent paintings by Michelangelo that adorn the ceiling of the Sistine Chapel. Yet the singer immediately adds that, despite his enchantment, he is not a Catholic but an ex-Catholic, and further that he found the experience claustrophobic. The latter comment surely has a double meaning: it is not just that the building felt too confining but that the religion itself is too narrow. So when we hear in "Rising Sun," a few songs later on the *Brainwashed* CD, about boundaries that cripple and people who have been programmed into guilt, we may well think specifically about Roman Catholic guilt and Roman Catholic parochialism.

As "P. 2. Vatican Blues (Last Saturday Night)" continues, we unfortunately enter a dark, conspiratorial view of the Roman Catholic church. "The truth," we are told, is "hiding" and "lurking." The nature of this ominous yet veiled truth becomes evident in the next rhyming word, "banking." The song endorses the naïve yet popular polemic that the Vatican, behind its pious façade of good will, is really a corrupt collection of power brokers who influence or direct world banking and governments for their own obscure but certainly selfish and sinister ends. The facts, the narrator says, are all too "suspicious," so much so that he felt compelled to inquire about the perplexing subject with a priest of his acquaintance. The one-size-fits-all answer he received in return from the priest was this: "One Our Father, three Hail Marys." The formulaic words are almost certainly from George's early life, perhaps from his so-called "first reconciliation," when he would have confessed his venial boyhood sins and would have been given, in consequence, a minimum, standard recipe for repentance—in this case saying The Lord's Prayer once and repeating a prayer to Mother Mary three times. The singer, in any case, is being instructed to atone for and forget his conspiratorial suspicions.

Yet he can't. Although he wishes the truth were otherwise, he knows better. Indeed, his obscure remark in the fourth verse about a "concrete tuxedo" might even be a play upon "concrete suit" or "concrete shoes" and so a reference to the Vatican's supposed Mafia connections. However that may be, "P. 2. Vatican Blues (Last Saturday Night)" oozes derision when, at 2:08 minutes into the song, one can, with the volume turned up, catch George's voice in the background penitently addressing a priest multiple times as "Father" and then, switching to the persona of the priest, charging the confessor to put some money in the box, so that everything will be OK.

George's scornful and sarcastic take on the Roman Catholic hierarchy doesn't appear for the first time on *Brainwashed*. It is already present on his earliest post-Beatles album, *All Things Must Pass*. In "Awaiting On You All," we are cautioned that whereas the Lord is about the business of helping human beings to wake up, the Pope is about the business of business. The Supreme Pontiff is in fact the majority shareholder in General Motors. Despite all his religious trappings, the Pope's wisdom and authority pertain solely to the stock exchange. So true liberation comes not from paying heed to Catholic teaching but rather, George offers, by chanting the names of God. We are not surprised when "Awaiting On You All" goes on to advise us that we can get along just fine without church buildings and rosary beads.

George's disrespect for Catholicism also takes visual form on the artwork for *Living In The Material World*. Inside the album there is a picture of George and six of his friends dining at a long table full of wine and good food. We clearly have here a parody of traditional depictions of the Last Supper. In George's mocking version, he stands up in the middle holding a glass of wine, dressed as a Roman Catholic priest—and he is clearly sporting a western six shooter. The photograph is seemingly a slam at the perceived materialism and violence of the Roman church.

Despite his early, unpleasant experiences in the Catholic Church and his lifelong alienation from it, George turned out to be, for whatever reason, ineradicably religious. Although he appears to have passed his teenage years without giving much thought to God, everything changed during the mid-1960s, when he was in his early twenties. It was then that he found himself attracted to Eastern religion, an attraction that soon became an obsession that greatly affected The Beatles and through them popular Western culture.

Although one sometimes reads that George and The Beatles were largely responsible for awakening the West to Indian religion, Indian dress, and Indian music, the truth is that the group's influential infatuation was rather the culmination of a lengthy historical process. Long before The Beatles appeared on the scene, the West had become more and more knowledgeable of and interested in the East. English translations of the sacred books of the eastern religions had become widely available by the opening of the twentieth century, and by then some were reading the theosophical works of Madame Blavatsky, who purported to reveal the mysterious wisdom of Tibet. In 1913, the Indian poet Rabindranath Tagore won not only the Nobel Prize for Literature but also a wide readership outside of his home country. The first several decades of the twentieth century also witnessed the fascinating and admirable life of Mahatma Gandhi, which stimulated a worldwide interest in Hinduism; and they further saw Swami Prabhavananda bring Vedanta to southern California and gain the public endorsement of Aldous Huxley. Likewise before the 1960s, Indra Devi moved to Hollywood, taught yoga to the stars, and wrote the first bestseller on yoga (*Forever Young, Forever Healthy*, 1953); and by then Indian restaurants had begun to pop up in the big European and American cities. So when The Beatles played the sitar, put on Nehru shirts, sat at the feet of a guru, and started chanting Indian mantras, they were not initiating a movement but rather adding momentum to one that was already well underway.

As for George himself, his own sympathy for Hinduism began not with the study of Indian religion but with listening to Indian music. In the Bahamas in early 1965, while they were making the movie *Help!*, The Beatles just happened to run into Swami Vishnu-devananda, founder of the International Sivananda Yoga Vedanta Centers and author of the well-known *The Complete Illustrated Book of Yoga* (1960). The Swami gave John, Paul, George, and Ringo each a little treatise on the philosophy of yoga. George later said that he paid it no heed at the time. He did, however, encounter the sitar for the first time while making *Help!* Indian musicians were on the set of the movie, and George and his bandmates enjoyed toying with the strange instrument. One can in fact see Paul holding a sitar in a scene in a restaurant.

Later in that same year in Los Angeles, immediately after The Beatles' tour of America, David Crosby and Roger McGuinn of The Byrds introduced George to the music of classical sitar maestro Ravi Shankar, and he was hooked. Shortly thereafter, for *Rubber Soul*, George played the sitar in Lennon's "Norwegian Wood (This Bird Has Flown)."[1] The next year, in April of 1966, he used the sitar on his own "Love You To" (*Revolver*), and on June 1 of that year, George met Ravi Shankar, whose records he by then knew well; he also saw him perform at the Royal Albert Hall. The two musicians immediately struck up a friendship, and George ever after claimed that he became interested in Hinduism only because Ravi Shankar was a Hindu. The friendship endured. George produced Ravi Shankar's *Chants Of India* in 1997; Shankar visited the former Beatle the day before he died; and Ravi Shankar's daughter, Anoushka, played the sitar in George's memory at *The Concert For George*.

After becoming captivated by Ravi Shankar, George took his next major stride into Hindusim when he accepted the sitar player's invitation to sojourn to Bombay and study the Indian instrument. In September of 1966, George did just that (and ended up pretty much neglecting his guitar for almost three years). The exotic atmosphere of India and the strange stories of holy men performing marvels fascinated George almost as much as the music. Part of the attraction was that he was tired of being a Beatle, and in India, without John, Paul, and Ringo, he discovered his own independent identity. In short order he became a believer in God, his songwriting matured, and he for once became the group's leader when the other Beatles later followed him on his return trip to India.

Several months after George had come back from India, Pattie Boyd, then his wife, introduced all The Beatles to Transcendental Meditation (TM). They found this a helpful and relatively easy way of dealing with the madness of their unrivalled fame, of dealing with what George likened to being "monkeys in a zoo"—so much so that they all famously decided, in February of 1968, to visit TM's founding guru, the Maharishi Mahesh Yogi, in his ashram in Rishikesh, India.

The story has often been told. The Maharishi, whom George had already met on an earlier trip to India, had pledged to them that, were they to follow his brand of meditation for only half an hour each day, they would be able to relax and find inner peace.

Although the time in India was musically productive—many of the songs on *The Beatles (The White Album)* and *Abbey Road* were composed there—Ringo didn't much like the food and didn't stay long, only about ten days. Paul had some success at meditation and remained longer, yet left India after five weeks. George and John, the most interested in what the Maharishi had to say, stayed only a couple of weeks longer. Rumors—George later said they were false—about the Maharishi bestowing inappropriate attentions upon female devotees brought disillusionment to Lennon, although perhaps by then he was only looking for an excuse to leave and get back to England so he could start his affair with Yoko Ono.

While George, like the other Beatles, left the Maharishi, the guru's teachings did not leave him. Not long after returning to England, George gave "Sour Milk Sea," a song he wrote in Rishikesh, to the Liverpool rocker, Jackie Lomax. It's an endorsement of TM, of what Lennon later called "instant karma." It opines that, if life has gone wrong, one can, without much trouble, make it right almost immediately. Although the song itemizes results—illumination, increased awareness, and release from limitation—instead of sketching the method for obtaining those results, it clearly promotes TM.

George's sympathy for TM's philosophy persisted throughout his life. As late as 1992, during the General U.K. Election, he joined a benefit concert for the Natural Law Party, a political faction of TM proponents. TM was, however, only one element in George's Hindu mixture. He was also strongly drawn to A. C. Bhaktivedanta Swami Prabhupāda (1896–1977) and the sectarian movement he founded, The International Society of Krisna Consciousness (ISKCON), whose adherents are popularly known as the Hare Krishnas. George indeed sometimes spoke of himself as a "closet Krishna," and he regularly gave copies of Prabhupāda's books to friends and acquaintances. He knew Prabhupāda personally, and he wrote "The Lord Loves The One (That Loves The Lord)" after a visit with the Swami. While the song names neither Prabhupāda nor ISKCON, it is a statement of the teachings that Prabhupāda highlighted for George upon that occasion: karma is the law of our existence; substituting ego for God is our problem; we must prepare ourselves for death.

Familiarity with the Hare Krishnas already shows up in John Lennon's "I Am The Walrus" (on The Beatles' 1967 *Magical Mystery Tour*), in the reference to their well-known chant.[2] George's own interest in the movement first displayed itself publicly in 1969, when he produced "The Hare Krishna Mantra," which was a hit in England and parts of Europe and Asia (although not in the U.S.). But it was only *All Things Must Pass* that publicly revealed the profundity of George's newfound devotion.

Prabhupāda taught the Hare Krishnas that the supreme personal God is Krishna, and that devotion to him will win enlightenment and liberation from the world. Such devotion includes chanting the Hare Krishna mantra: "Hare (= Lord) Krishna, Hare Krishna, Krishna, Krishna, Hare Hare/Hare Rama (like Krishna, one of the incarnations of Lord Vishnu), Hare Rama, Rama Rama, Hare Hare." George managed to work the first twelve words of this sixteen-word mantra into the second half of "My Sweet Lord," where it conspicuously replaces the responsory "hallelujah" in the first half. Chanting to Krishna is also prominently featured in "It Is He (Jai Sri Krishna)," on *Dark Horse*, where George repeatedly praises his Lord with "Jai (= Hail!) Krishna." George learned the lengthy chant to which these words belong when he was in Brindaban, India, a center of devotion to Krishna, and his lyrics offer his own loose English translation of the Indian original.[3]

The extent of George's lifelong dedication to the Hare Krishna cause appears from several telling facts:

* In 1969 he helped refurbish a building in London for an ISKCON temple.
* That same year Apple signed the Radha Krishna Temple as a recording act, out of which came the recording, "The Hare Krishna Mantra."
* He helped pay for the publication of Prabhupāda's *Krsna: The Supreme Personality of the Godhead* (1970), to which he also contributed the preface.

- The artwork for George's *Living In The Material World* (1973) features a picture of Krishna taken from Prabhupāda's edition of the *Bhagavad-Gita*.
- In 1973, George donated an English Tudor mansion on a seventeen-acre site, a mansion which he had used as a studio, to the Hare Krishnas. It became a large international center.
- During his 1974 American tour, George induced his audiences to chant the Hare Krishna mantra. That same year he went to the holy Indian city, Brindaban, a pilgrimage site of devotion to Krishna as shepherd.
- Krishna is floating above all the people on the cover of *Dark Horse* (1974).
- In 1982 George agreed to meet with and answer the questions of Mukunda Goswami, a leading spokesperson for the Hare Krishnas and the man who had earlier introduced the Beatle to Prabhupāda in 1969. During their conversation, George enthusiastically endorsed ISKCON's beliefs and practices. The organization still proudly carries the very informative interview on its website.[4]
- George was a prominent figure at the 1997 celebration of the Hare Krishnas at the Bhaktivedanta Manor, which George had purchased for them twenty-five years before.
- When attacked in 1999, George reportedly cried out, "Hare Krishna."
- Hare Krishna devotees visited with George shortly before he died, and ISKCON temples commemorated his passing. (Early reports that he had made provisions for ISKCON in his will, however, turned out to be unfounded. He left the entirety of his estate to his wife and son, Dhani.)

Consistent with George's commitment to ISKCON teachings, the earnest "Awaiting On You All," on *All Things Must Pass*, repeatedly commends chanting the names of God, promising that the act will bring spiritual freedom. Although the song fails to elaborate, George supplied commentary elsewhere. In various interviews he spoke about chanting as a way of remembering God and staying in tune with reality, about his desire to chant whenever possible, and about his experience of spiritual bliss and feeling of God's presence while chanting. In one particular interview he added the theological proposition that "the word 'Hare' calls upon the energy of the Lord. If you chant the mantra enough, you build up an identification with God. God's all happiness, all bliss, and by chanting His name we connect with Him. So it's really a process of actually having God realization, which becomes clear with the expanded state of consciousness that develops when you chant."[5] It seems altogether fitting that the very last song ("Brainwashed") on George's very last album (*Brainwashed*) ends with his chanting. He bids us farewell by repeating the name of the God Shiva and epithets for him.

Perhaps it bears remarking, in passing, that the chanting that ends *Brainwashed* is the most explicit statement of Hindu religiosity on any song since "It Is He (Jai Sri Krishna)" on *Dark Horse* in the mid-1970s. We should probably relate this circumstance to reflections George offered in 1982: "Back in the sixties, whatever we were all getting into, we tended to broadcast it loud as we could. I had had certain realizations and went through a period where I was so thrilled about my discoveries and realizations that I wanted to shout and tell it to everybody. But there's a time to shout it out and a time not to shout it out."[6] One infers that, when making *All Things Must Pass*, *Living In The Material World*, and *Dark Horse*, which in two cases literally wear their Hinduism on their record sleeves, George wanted to shout. When he later made *Thirty Three & 1/3*, *George Harrison*, *Somewhere In England*, *Gone Troppo*, and *Cloud Nine*, he thought it more prudent to lower his voice: the religious message remains, but it is less prominent, more subdued. The uninhibited *Brainwashed*, however, reverts to the extroverted faith of the early George. The religious themes are again recurrent, and once more George chants to his Hindu Deity. One presumes that he knew that this was his last opportunity to communicate his faith to the world at large, his last blast, and it was time again to trumpet his convictions.

Before leaving discussion of George's debts to particular Hindu teachers and movements and how they are reflected in his music, mention should be made of his affection for Paramhansa Yogananda (who already appears as one of the famous faces on the cover of *Sgt. Pepper's Lonely Hearts Club Band*). In his autobiography, George tells us that "Dear One," on *Thirty-Three & 1/3*, was composed for Yogananda, "a great influence on my life."[7] Yogananda was the author of the influential *Autobiography of a Yogi*—the book's many miraculous tales no doubt appealed to George's fondness for exotic gurus—as well as the founder of Self-Realisation Fellowship and the first prominent yogi to take up residence in the United States. The song itself, a happy declaration of love, is presumably directed to God, to the "Dear One" whom George loves, although George was sufficiently practiced at ambiguity that the words may be at the same time a prayer to the dead Yogananda to bestow his spirit of love and truth upon George. The song was written in 1976, and it seems to reflect George's renewal after his "naughty period." The second line laconically follows the word "reborn" with the compound "worldwise," implying that the singer has learned his lesson about life in the world and has found his true, religious self again. The very next words are, "mind at rest." The period of worldly turmoil has ended; the "Dear One" is the center of life once more—and perhaps, it is suggested, this timely recovery of lived faith had something to do with returning to the teachings of Yogananda.

Despite George's support of various Hindu groups and temples, he remained, as he said, religiously in the closet; that is, he did not publicly identify himself with one and only one religious group. In line with this, although he did sometimes attend Hindu temples, he appears to have practiced his piety mostly on his own, chanting and meditating and contemplating by himself. Those close to him tell us that he practiced meditation throughout life,[8] sometimes several hours a day; they do not inform us that he regularly entered any one religious building for public worship. In this respect, his music reflects his biography, for it addresses not communal religiosity—which, to be fair to George, may have been well nigh impossible, given his fame, for him to participate in[9]—but the religious individual.

"Awaiting On You All" is unequivocal: it tells us that we have no need to attend a "church house" or to visit a "temple," because what matters is the heart. (Perhaps one should compare *Vishnu Purana* 6.2.17: "In this age there is no use in meditation, sacrifice and temple worship; by simply chanting the holy name of Krishna ... one can achieve perfect self-realization.") Like so many modern western people, George believed that authentic religion is *really* personal religion, not collective practice. (A 1995–96 survey of Americans reported that about a third believe that "people have God within them, so churches aren't necessary.") What he craved was an intense, personal relationship with God, direct, authentic, unmediated. For this, he believed, neither a formal organization nor a professionally trained religious leader was required. Indeed, religious institutions can be full of hypocrites. "Any Road" speaks of those who acknowledge God as "Sir" and yet don't know the road they are supposed to be traveling—which is reminiscent of the Sermon on the Mount, where some say "Lord, Lord" but travel down the easy road that leads to destruction (Matt 7:13–21). The image in "Pisces Fish," of a church bell ringer getting tangled up in his rope, is surely another way of expressing ecclesiastical deficiency. There is nothing in George's music about what happens when two or three are gathered together for a religious end. George even disparaged organized Hinduism when he met nominal attendees who knew less about their native faith than he did. The personal matters more than the institutional; in the current jargon, we should be spiritual, which doesn't necessarily mean being religious.

The relative paucity of participation in communal practices or in any specific organized religion goes back to George's teenage years. It also marks a point of continuity with the lyrics of The Beatles' "Eleanor Rigby."[10] In this a priest preaches to empty pews, a lonely woman dies and is forgotten, and nobody gets saved. The sense of the whole is that the public Christian or Catholic church is a dead institution.

At this juncture perhaps we should pay some attention to George's complex relationship to John Lennon, which remains puzzling precisely because of the intensity of George's religious devotion. Lennon seemingly spoke against everything that George held dear,[11] and yet the latter never ceased to idolize the former and commend his musical message. How do we explain this?

While George, as we have seen, could be very critical of institutional religion, especially of Roman Catholicism, he had a profound faith in God, and his religious convictions were the central element in his personal biography. John, by contrast, publicly assailed not only organized Western religion but also denounced Eastern religious traditions, and his music explicitly denies the existence of God as well as the reality of an afterlife. Maybe Lennon's "I Am The Walrus," which seems to mock the mechanical chanting of the Hare Krishnas ("Elementary penguin singing Hare Krishna"), was not heartfelt, and maybe "Sexy Sadie" was a denunciation of the Maharishi in particular, not of Hinduism in general, but "Imagine" is another matter. This exquisite piano piece, unfortunately overlaid by sophomoric sentiments, asks us to imagine a utopia where there is no religion, no heaven, no hell. The invitation seems to be a denial of transcendent realities. All that counts, and all that we should be concerned with, lies in this world.

Lennon was not always so cynical. His infamous comment about The Beatles being more popular than Jesus Christ, published in *The Evening Standard* on March 4, 1966, really wasn't a statement of utter unbelief, because it was immediately followed by this: "Jesus was all right, but his disciples were thick and ordinary. It's them twisting it that ruins it for me." So when Lennon—because of the uproar in the United States, not England—later apologized, explaining that he wasn't putting down religion, and that he wasn't "anti-God, anti-Christ, or anti-religion," his self-serving comments may not have been wholly tendentious.

In later years, however, after his disillusionment in India, he penned songs that are indeed anti-God, anti-Christ, and anti-religion; the irreligious ideology of "Imagine" hardly stands by itself. In "God," from the album *John Lennon/Plastic Ono Band* (1970), Lennon offers that the Supreme Spirit is a human construct with which we console ourselves, and he gives us an inventory of things in which he doesn't believe, including the Bible, Jesus, Buddha, mantras, the *Bhagavad-Gita*, and yoga.

One can hardly regard this catalog of disbelief, which bluntly dismisses much that George held dear, as an anomaly in the Lennon musical corpus. "I Found Out," on *John Lennon/Plastic Ono Band* (1970), is also a scathing rejection of religious faith. It proclaims that Jesus will not return from heaven, that "Old Hare Krishna" delivers nothing except "pie in the sky," that gurus don't know more truth than the rest of us, and that religion is nothing but an opiate.

More of the same turns up on home recordings released in 1998 on the *John Lennon Anthology*. "Serve Yourself," a polemical response to

THE LOVE THERE THAT'S SLEEPING

Bob Dylan's Christian "You Gotta Serve Somebody," belittles faith in Jesus Christ, Buddha, Mohammed, and Krishna, and it contemptuously associates religion with wars. "The Great Wok" dismisses eastern asceticism and professes indifference about wisdom from the Himalayas. "The Rishi Kesh Song" ridicules as naïve the expectation that a mantra, a "little word," will resolve life's questions.

Given such recurrent sentiments as these, it is truly curious to listen to the pious George eulogizing the doubting John in "All Those Years Ago" (which rose to the number two spot on the U.S. charts in 1981). This lightweight hit, whose sober subject matter hardly suits the bouncy tune,[12] does more than celebrate a friendship: it also presents John as a wholly admirable, persecuted prophet. Although treated like a dog, the enlightened musician, according to George, instructed us as to how we should give and love. George further tells us that he "always looked up to" John. One might diminish the force of this by noting the past tense, as though George once looked up to John but doesn't any longer. But that would betray the admiration than runs through the whole song, and it would leave unexplained how George can go on to confess that, when things are dark, he can find himself praying to John, who is now in "the world of light." It would also contradict George's public statement upon John's death: "I had and still have great love and respect for him."

All this is strange enough. Matters become even stranger when George commends John as the one who, once upon a time, "imagined it all." This is a transparent allusion to the famous song, "Imagine." George is affectionately recalling lyrics that undermine his most precious beliefs. The paradox continues when, in the middle of praising John, George complains that people have forgotten God, apart from whom there is no reason for anything. But John not only apparently forgot God: he consciously repudiated God. So when "All Those Years Ago" approaches its end by asserting that most people did not have ears to hear what John was really saying, one has to wonder about George's own sense of hearing.

We can hardly suppose that George mistook John's antagonism to religious belief and behavior as directed solely at organized religion, nor is it plausible that George interpreted John's vicious barbs as ill considered, nothing but expressions of passing feelings, not deeply meant. The hostility is too far-reaching and too heartfelt to be thus mitigated. A better guess is that, on George's reckoning, John preached enough truth that the attacks on religion could be conveniently overlooked. We know that people in mourning often idealize the dead and rewrite memories for the better. The eulogy is more than a formal convention: it reflects the strong human inclination to think the best of the dead. Moreover, the title, "All Those Years Ago," may intimate that, despite the allusion to "Imagine," George is primarily remembering John in his pre-Yoko days, or John before his disillusionment with the Maharishi, or John before his post-Beatles melancholy.

There is also an additional factor to consider. Maybe George knew—even though he evidently didn't visit John during the last five years of the latter's life—or maybe George hoped that his old friend's enmity toward religion softened over the years, that the animosity of the late 1960s and early 1970s grew into a more mature receptivity. Lennon's mind was certainly inconstant on a host of issues. What he thought at one time is no indicator of what he thought at another. His political views, for example, were scarcely consistent. So we can at least ask whether we should understand his rebuffs of religion, many of which predate his death by a decade, as necessarily his last word.

Leaving aside the controversial claim of a couple of authors that, in 1976 or 1977, John had a short-lived conversion to evangelical Christianity,[13] a hint perhaps that he changed his mind might lie in "Grow Old With Me," versions of which appeared on the posthumous *Milk And Honey* (1984) and *John Lennon Anthology* (1998). This love song, which Mary Chapin Carpenter covered, and which became for a time popular at weddings, repeats "God bless our love" a full six times. Although one can deem the refrain nothing but a traditional phrase without real meaning, it remains unexpected given Lennon's one-time conscious and explicit atheism. Do the words then betray a relaxation of opposition toward religion? That they do seems established by Lennon's "Help Me To Help Myself," one of his last recordings (later included on the remastered 2000 version of *Double Fantasy*). Here John, after quoting the old saying, "The Lord helps those who help themselves," goes on to confess that he has never been satisfied. He then prays directly to God and repeatedly asks God to help him. This is not the atheist of earlier albums.

In line with this, Lennon said the following in 1980, in the last interview he granted: "People always got the image I was an anti-Christ or anti-religion. I'm not. I'm a most religious fellow. I was brought up a Christian and I only now understand some of the things that Christ was saying in those parables. Because people got hooked on the teacher and missed the message."[14] This is quite an arresting statement. It is unfortunate that the interviewer, perhaps shying from the topic, immediately changed the subject, so that the implications remain unclarified for us. The standard Lennon biographies likewise fail us here, for while they inform us that John and Yoko were passionate about magic, astrology, numerology, and tarot cards and so were anything but modern materialistic skeptics, they are not much interested in explicating the course of Lennon's varying religious sentiments.

It is intriguing that George, shortly after John's death, not only assured us that his old friend was in a better place, but also attributed to him a belief in karma and reincarnation.[15] One would like to know if George really had this information from the post-Beatle John himself and, if not, why he felt justified in making the comment.[16] One would also like to know whether George took solace from Yoko Ono's public comment on the meaning of "Help Me To Help Myself," which she offered very shortly after John's murder: "They say that people start to think of God near death. It's possible that was the case here."

However one resolves George's abiding and seemingly unqualified commendation of John's music, which dismisses beliefs dear to George's heart, on one matter there is undoubted continuity between the two men, or at least between George and John's remark that, while he didn't mind Jesus, the church had got things wrong and gone astray. The post-1967 George, in his own mind, never rejected Jesus himself, only some forms of Christianity.

We have already seen that George was hostile to Roman Catholicism. He was also unhappy with Protestant fundamentalism. His final composition, "Horse To Water," which appeared on Jools Holland's *Small World, Big Band* (2001), derides a preacher who warns about the devil and yet himself seems possessed, a man who prefers to rail against fornication instead of promoting "God realization." The target is obviously Christian fundamentalism.

George's discomfort with so much of official Christianity did not, however, extend to its founder. He once called Jesus Christ "an absolute yogi," and he then added this: "I think many Christian teachers today are misrepresenting Christ. They're supposed to be representing Jesus, but they're not doing it very well. They're letting him down very badly, and that's a big turnoff."[17] These words enshrine a positive evaluation of Jesus himself, as does George's music. "Awaiting On You All," for example, informs us that, if we open up our hearts, we will be able to see Jesus because he is always right there, waiting to relieve us of our cares. Similarly, "Life Itself" affirms that the names of God include Jehovah and Christ.[18] So when "My Sweet Lord" intermingles "Hallelujah" with "Hare Krishna," the composer's intention is obvious. He is not cynically replacing an empty biblical expression with a better Hindu expression. He is rather communicating that the divine reality known to Hindus as Krishna is the same reality that appeared in western history in Jesus Christ.[19]

That George was sincere about this conviction is confirmed by the fact that, in 1969, he told an interviewer that he had come to understand what Jesus was all about through Hinduism. It is telling that, in real life, he often signed letters not just with an Eastern religious symbol but also with a cross. This same combination now appears on the cover of the boxed set of *The Dark Horse Years 1976–1992*.

In finding God in Jesus as well as Krishna, George was not just following the lazy eclecticism so typical of our modern world, with its generous acceptance of pluralism, its embracing of all different styles and tastes, and its indifference to genuine contradiction. George's ecumenism was rather a studied doctrine learned from his modern Hindu teachers. He had been indoctrinated into Vedanta-based movements, which have typically found golden threads in the tattered tapestries of all the world's major religions and so have promoted religious toleration. Already the *Rig Veda* says that "Truth is one, although sages call it by different names," and modern Hindu leaders have applied this to the major religions of the world. Swami Prabhavananda used to say that if one were to put the followers of Jesus, Buddha, and Mohammad into the same room, they would kill each other, but that if those three men found themselves in the same room they would embrace one another. Paramahansa Yogananda similarly taught that there is a "complete harmony and basic oneness of original Christianity as taught by Jesus Christ and original Yoga as taught by Bhagavan Krishna."[20] George thought the same, and even accepted what Bhaktivedanta Swami Prabhupāda taught the Hare Krishnas to believe, that the Greek word for Christ, *Christos*, is the same word as Krishna, which some Indians pronounce as "Krsta." For George, as for the Hare Krishnas, Jesus Christ was, like Lord Krishna, an avatar, a supreme manifestation or incarnation of the Divinity, one of the "saviors throughout time" (to use the expression on "Tears Of The World").[21]

With all this in mind, it is no surprise to learn that, shortly after his death, one of his good friends asserted that George was much interested in Eastern versions of Christianity, that he studied apocryphal gospels such as the Gospel of Thomas, and that he "very much had a relationship with Christ."[22] If this is indeed the truth—and we have no reason to doubt that it is—then we might anticipate that George's music might reflect some knowledge of the Bible, and especially the gospels. Certainly it is hard to imagine that a man who was curious about the noncanonical gospels had no interest whatsoever in their biblical counterparts; and the evidence is that George did in fact have such an interest. I have noticed the following clear allusions to biblical passages appearing in Harrisongs:

- The words on "Brainwashed," "A voice cries in the wilderness," are originally from a prophecy in Isaiah 40:3. Matthew 3:3; Mark 1:3; and Luke 3:4 cite this oracle and in each instance apply it to John the Baptist. The same prophetic line occurs at the end of the CD booklet for *Brainwashed*, as a caption in one of George's own drawings (with the misspelling "cry's," which should be "cries").

- "The Day The World Gets 'Round" uses the phrase, "the pure in heart." The phrase is from the famous beatitude in Matthew's gospel: "Blessed are the pure in heart, for they will see God."

- In "Love Comes To Everyone," George pledges, "Knock and it will open wide." This is close to Matthew 7:7 and Luke 11:9: "Knock, and the door will be opened for you." George without question knew that the words come from Jesus, for at a press conference in Los Angeles in 1974 he said, with reference to his own spiritual journey, "I remembered Jesus said somewhere, 'Knock and the door shall be opened' and I said, 'Knock, knock. Hello!'"

- In the song entitled "If You Believe," George sings that "everything you thought is possible." This is probably an echo of Jesus' promise, recorded in different forms in Matthew 17:20; 21:21–22; Mark 11:22–24; and Luke 17:6, that, if one has faith and believes, "nothing will be impossible for you," and of the correlative proposition, appearing in Matthew 19:26; Mark 9:23; 10:27; and 14:36, that with God "all things are possible."
- The obscure "Lay His Head," the B-side of "Got My Mind Set On You," says that "sometimes a man, he has nowhere to lay his head." This echoes the saying in Matthew 8:20 and Luke 9:58: "Foxes have holes, and birds of the air have nests; but the Son of Man has nowhere to lay his head." According to *The Beatles' Anthology*, George called this saying to mind when he found that even in India he was famous and a magnet for crowds. He thought to himself: "Foxes have holes and birds have nests, but the Beatles have nowhere to lay their heads."[23]
- "Unconsciousness Rules" speaks of "blind leading the blind," a phrase occurring in Matthew 15:14 and Luke 6:39.
- "Within You Without You" refers to people "who gain the world and lose their soul." This takes up the language of Matthew 16:26 and Mark 8:36.
- The title for "Writing's On The Wall" comes from Daniel 5.
- The words, "Reaping what you sow," on the little-known song, "Mo," recalls several New Testament texts: Matthew 25:24, 26; Luke 19:21–22; John 4:36–37; 1 Corinthians 9:11; 2 Corinthians 9:6; Galatians 6:7–8.

Some of these phrases, such as "blind leading the blind," "the writing's on the wall," and "reaping what you sow," are sufficiently common in our popular western culture that utilizing them requires no firsthand acquaintance with the Bible. This is, however, hardly the case with all of the turns of phrase just listed. And in a couple of instances, as already noted, we have George's own testimony that he knew the source of an expression or sentence to be Jesus. With only one exception, moreover, the relevant verses are all from the Gospels. This is significant because the supposition that George paid more attention to the Gospels than to the rest of Christian Scripture makes perfect sense. While Jesus was, in George's theology, an avatar, the disciples got some important things mixed up. Such a belief would encourage one to pay much more attention to the Gospels than to any other portion of the Bible, and it is precisely a knowledge of the Gospels, not the rest of the Bible, that appears reflected in George's lyrics.[24]

Although there is not enough evidence to show that George knew the canonical Gospels well, there is enough evidence to show that he knew something of their content; and because, in each instance cited above, the material borrowed from the Gospels is put to positive use and so reflects a sympathetic reading, we have here more evidence that, although George rejected Roman Catholicism and Protestant fundamentalism, he did not reject Jesus.

In spite of the critical distance from his Christian childhood, George never wholly abandoned the religion of his youth and of his mother because he never, in his own mind, abandoned Jesus, only Jesus' misinterpreters. It is intriguing in this connection that George used Japa meditation beads—this is the real subject, he claimed, of "Awaiting On You All"[25]—which have their obvious counterpart in the prayer beads of Roman Catholic devotion; that George selected a faith that encouraged a positive interpretation of Jesus Christ; and that George fell in love with Lord Krishna, who is probably the most Christlike of all the Hindu divinities. In the end, George's adopted adult faith retained significant links of both practice and belief with his abandoned boyhood religion. Notwithstanding all the bad memories, he believed, as he put it in a 1974 press conference, that "Jesus is on the mainline."

Notes

1. Independently of *Rubber Soul*, The Kinks used the sound of the Indian sitar in their 1965 release, "See My Friends." Whether or not this was the first

rock record to employ a sitar, there was clearly something in the air. Although The Kinks may have become interested in the sitar when making a stop in India on their way to a gig in Australia, one also wonders whether some rock and rollers were paying attention to the experimental music of jazzist John Coltrane. Under the influence of Ravi Shankar, Coltrane was then incorporating Indian sounds into his music.

2. Lennon, whose memory was not always accurate, later claimed the words were aimed firstly at Allen Ginsberg and those like him, not the Hare Krishnas as such.

3. George tells the story in *I, Me, Mine* (San Francisco: Chronicle Books, 2002), 296–97.

4. Available online at: www.krishna.org/Articles/2000/08/00066.html. There are, however, stories of George distancing himself from ISKCON devotees in the 1980s.

5. Taken from a 1982 interview by Mukunda Goswami, available online at: www.krishna.org/Articles/2000/08/00066.html. For similar thoughts see Harrison, *I, Me, Mine*, 200.

6. Taken from a 1982 interview by Mukunda Goswami, available online at: www.krishna.org/Articles/2000/08/00066.html.

7. Harrison, *I, Me, Mine*, 326.

8. Although he admitted in his 1974 L.A. press conference that he hadn't "sat down and done meditation for some time." This statement tellingly comes from a period of significant personal crisis.

9. Once, while worshipping at the ISCKON temple in London, his shoes were stolen. After that, those in charge made sure that, when George went to the temple, others were dismissed. Lennon's assassination, which left George frightened and according to some almost paranoid, must have made matters even worse.

10. The lyricist is disputed. Paul remembers that he was the main writer. According to Yoko Ono, John claimed to be the chief author.

11. Lennon—who said once that he and George had a "love-hate relationship"—also publicly complained about George's *I, Me, Mine*: he was hurt that he is so much in the background.

12. The explanation for the incongruity between lyrical content and musical form may be due to the circumstance that George originally intended the song for Ringo and then rewrote it after Lennon's murder, although there are certainly other Harrisongs in which the lyrics and the music are an odd match.

13. Geoffrey Giuliano, *Lennon in America* (New York: Cooper Square Press, 2000), and Robert Rosen, *Nowhere Man: The Final Days of John Lennon* (San Francisco: Last Gasp, 2002).

14. Available online at: john-lennon.com/playboyinterviewwithjohnlennonandyokoono.htm1980.

15. Taken from a 1982 interview by Mukunda Goswami, available online at: www.krishna.org/Articles/2000/08/00066.html.

16. For remarks from John of similar import, allegedly made during the last year of his life, see Frederic Seaman, *The Last Days of John Lennon: A Personal Memoir* (New York: Birch Lane, 1991), 189.

17. Taken from a 1982 Interview by Mukunda Goswami, available online at: www.krishna.org/Articles/2000/08/00066.html. In the same interview he caricatures most Christian churches as being morbid because they are too somber and deny the possibility of seeing God in the here and now; they instead teach their adherents: "He's way up above you. Just believe what we tell you and shut up." One may compare George's defense of the movie, *Life of Brian*, which some thought sacrilegious: "Myself and all of Monty Python have great respect for Christ. . . . Actually it was upholding Him and knocking all the idiotic stuff that goes on around religion. . . ." See Elliot J. Huntley, *Mystical One: George Harrison after the Breakup of the Beatles* (Toronto: Guernica, 2004), 157.

18. Cf. George's Preface to *Krsna*: "Allah-Buddha-Jehova-Rama: All are Krsna, all are One."

19. The Beatles had long ago used "Hallelujah" in a song they performed and recorded but, before *Anthology*, never put on an album: "Hallelujah, I Love Her So." In this the word has no religious sense.

20. Paramahansa Yogananda, *Autobiography of a Yogi* (Los Angeles: Self-Realization Fellowship, 1990), 573.

21. Cf. Harrison, *I, Me, Mine*, 181: Christ suffered and "took on others' Karma in his own body as the 'Saviour.'"

22. See the interview of Deepak Chopra at: www.beliefnet.com/story/94/story_9434.html.

23. The Beatles, *The Beatles' Anthology* (Chronicle Books, 2000), 223.

24. I note, however, that, in Harrison, *I, Me, Mine*, 180, George quotes the King James Version of Galatians 6:7 ("God is not mocked: for whatsoever a man soweth, that shall he also reap") and correctly cites its source.

25. Harrison, *I, Me, Mine*, 200.

5

The Material World

OUR PREDICAMENT

"The material world" is, in George's music, a pejorative phrase, and in the song, "Living In The Material World," he observes that we spend our days not in happiness but in frustration. Life wears us out, and we can go utterly astray. But why should this be so? What is wrong with the world?

George tells us that, for one thing, the material world constantly teases our senses with false promises. It abounds with things that we all long to possess; and yet, once we have them, we remain unsatisfied, our material thirsts unquenched. Indeed, the more we have, the more we seem to want, as the wealthy George knows all too well. It follows that our senses will never be "gratified." They will, rather, constantly swell "like a tide."

The sentiment shows up not only in "Living In The Material World" but also on *Somewhere In England*, in the catchy "Unconsciousness Rules."

Here again George, sounding a little like the Buddha and a little like the Catholic apologist Blaise Pascal, admonishes us that the physical "senses," no matter what they hanker after and obtain, remain "unsatisfied." But what, he is implicitly asking us, is the point of trying to satisfy those senses? What is the use of striving after material things that only leave us wanting more? As George sings in "Simply Shady," this is a "madness" that always craves for "more."

If each individual is ill with the fire of misplaced desire, it follows that society, the collection of individuals, must likewise be sick, and this in fact is a second problem with the material world. In his 1974 Los Angeles press conference, George admitted that, while most imagine that the world as a whole will someday "get itself together," so that "we'll all be okay," he doubted that this would ever happen. He did not expect the material world to transform itself into utopia, either sooner or later. His only real hope was that individuals, one by one, would eventually liberate themselves from the chains of karma. The material world is only the arena for the redemption of individual souls, who burn out their attachment to it one at a time. It can be the vestibule to a better place, but it cannot be that place. So nobody can save the world. As George sings in "That Which I Have Lost," the best that we are probably able to do is to become enlightened, that is, obtain consciousness of God for ourselves. Then we can share this miraculous discovery with others, in the hope that they might obtain it, too.

Yet a third difficulty with this material world is that everything in it is transient. In "Writing's On The Wall," from *Somewhere In England*, George remarks how strange it is that, as death continues to draw nearer to us with each passing day, we latch onto things "that have no grace or power." We're always grasping for and trying to hold on to material things even as they fade before our eyes. This makes no sense. In a particularly poignant illustration, George remarks that even friendships, which we rightly value so much, don't last because we all must die. "All Things Must Pass" is all-inclusive: everything in this material world, including all of us, is destined to make an exit. As George memorably puts it, "none of life's strings can last." That is, human beings are like guitar strings, which must be periodically replaced because they don't last forever. Moreover, George feels that to perish is to lose worth, and that, to the contrary, to endure is to increase worth. So the ultimate or absolute value, if there is any, must be or must belong to some enduring realm beyond this ever-dissipating material world.

That the material world is transient, that it can never morph into utopia, and that it is full of false promises are more than generalizations drawn from George's own experience. He is not just reporting to us on what he has seen; he is equally sharing with us religious doctrine that he has been taught. It is basic Hindu teaching that, regarding the true nature of our own existence and of things in the material world generally, our mundane senses lead us seriously astray. This conviction comes to explicit expression in "Beware Of Darkness," in which George warns listeners about *mâya*, illusion. Historically, the concept has been tied to the notion that the whole world is a grand chimera, to which we foolishly attach ourselves through our thirsting senses. Failing to exercise discrimination, we become affixed to the unreal, to that which seems to be but in truth isn't. As George puts it in "That Which I Have Lost," "the dust of desire" obscures the divine light. He agrees with the Vedic Scriptures, which teach "that the physical world operates under one fundamental law of *mâya*, the principle of relativity and duality. God, the Sole Life, is Absolute Unity; to appear as the separate and diverse manifestations of a creation He wears a false or unreal veil. That illusory dualistic veil is *mâya*."[1] It's all a bit like what our physicists now tell us—a fact Hindu apologists haven't missed—that subatomic physics has dissolved the reality, that we live in a world of shadows, that the solidity of objects is illusory, that things are made up of mostly empty space.

George consistently expounds this view of things. In his music, our ordinary senses are limited to perceiving this tangible, visible material world; and as there is another and much more important world beyond what we see and hear and touch—he calls this "the higher world" on "That Which I Have Lost"—our earthbound senses typically become our foes rather than our friends. Appearances are against the truth, so that *mâya* rules the world. As we accordingly hear on *All Things Must Pass*, in the "Ballad Of Sir Frankie Crisp (Let It Roll)," the "illusions" of fools are "everywhere."

In "Living In The Material World," George, recalling his time as a Beatle, confesses that he too was once "caught up in the material world"; and in "Simply Shady," he recalls a time when he was "blinded by desire." He now knows, however, how empty his life was because he knows how empty this life is. He acknowledges that, however grand and glorious they may have been in the eyes of others, his pursuits and achievements with John, Paul, and Ringo did not bring meaningful contentment, and he now realizes that his true home is elsewhere, in the "spiritual sky." So his goal is to get from here to there. That is why "Living In The Material World" ends with George's expressing the hope that he will eventually leave the world through the grace of Lord Krsna, and why, in another song, "I Live For You," he can declare that he doesn't have a care for this world. This is his version of the refrain in Ecclesiastes' "All is vanity." As he said in his 1982 interview with Mukunda Goswami, "This place's not really what's happening. We don't belong here, but in the spiritual sky." Again, "the whole point to being here, really, is to figure a way to get out."[2]

This interpretation of the world as a grand illusion that needs to be exposed for what it is, or rather for what it is not, is central to George's view of things. It is anticipated already in "Within You Without You," his 1967 contribution to *Sgt. Pepper's Lonely Hearts Club Band*. Here George reflects at length upon the human subjection to misperception. He contemplates people—there is no reason to think that he excludes himself from their company—who "hide themselves behind a wall of illusion." These are people who die before they find the truth, who fail to understand and hold onto love. They don't see that the resources for happiness and authentic change are within themselves; instead, they have been duped into blaming others or circumstances for what they lack. If they ever do finally gain the world, which is what they think they want, then they will lose their souls. Peace of mind escapes them because they can't see beyond themselves, can't see that "we're all one."

Although "Within You Without You" is heavily indebted to Indian music, it is unclear whether George's assertion that "we're all one" is a full-blooded, self-conscious affirmation of the Hindu doctrine of the One behind the many or, more simply, a humanistic avowal that people are pretty much the same under their different skins and cultures. So George's Hinduism here remains inchoate. Later recordings are less ambiguous, one example being "Mâya Love," on

Dark Horse. This is a meditation, presumably informed by his failed first marriage, upon love that is unreal. The singer informs us that there is a sort of love that is like the sea insofar as it comes and goes. It is like the day in that it gives way to night. And it is like the wind when it blows too hard and becomes a danger. All this presumably stands in contrast to God's love, which doesn't come and go, which never gives way to night, and which heals rather than harms.

"Mâya Love" ends by referring to "this cosmic dream," and this is just another way of expressing George's Hindu belief that the material world is an illusion, nothing more than God's dream. The metaphor recurs in "Unknown Delight," where the singer meditates upon the "angel," his newborn son, Dhani, who has come into his "dream." In other words, George here conceptualizes his existence in this world as a dream.

This is not just a passing feeling or a throwaway description; it is instead a foundational metaphysical conviction. In the bouncy "Dream Away," written for the movie *Time Bandits*, George ends with the words, "sharing a dream with you." This is a way of saying that he is not alone: we all live in *mâya*, in God's cosmic dream, in the world of illusion. And when he goes on cryptically to comment that there is an astounding "mystery," and that its "handiworks" are "only a dream away," he seems to be telling us that what lies between individuals and the spiritual reality that they need is only an illusion, only *mâya*. This hints that there is a way of passing beyond the fleeting appearances, to something that is not illusory. We shall take up this subject in chapter 6.

But the sad truth is that, according to George's thought, and in accord with his belief in the ruling power of *mâya*, most individuals have not passed beyond the illusion; they mistake the unreal for the real, and vice versa. They know neither that the world is a mirage nor that what matters is invisible to our ordinary senses. People are instead attached to this material world, to transient things that do not fulfill their deepest needs. They are, then, not really awake; they are dreaming as they slumber. From one point of view, George has a very gloomy take on the human condition. Most of us live out our lives in ignorance of the material world's true nature and unaware of our own spiritual poverty. For, as the *Bhagavad-Gita* says regarding *mâya*, "It is hard to pierce the divine veil that consists of the various spectacles that hide Me" (7:14).

It is no surprise, then, that George so often depicts the world as a dark place (which is the setting in which we usually dream). The gloomy "Beware Of Darkness" is representative. Along with its repeated admonitions to "watch out" and "take care," it offers a catalog of things to shun—swingers, greedy political leaders, big business selling its wares, and crippling thoughts that beget hopelessness. George insists that these vain things, which seem to be something but are not, prevent us from accomplishing what we're here to accomplish. They are channels of darkness that stunt the growth of our true natures. In one of his most memorable similes, he compares people to Weeping Atlas Cedars, evergreen trees whose nature it is to grow. The comparison is apt at every level. Because we are not fulfilling our true end, we are sad and miserable; we accordingly weep. Because we pass our everyday lives on the material plain, we are like the weary Atlas of Greek mythology, who carried the weight of the entire heavens on his back; we are overburdened. And we are like cedars, which are by nature inclined to grow to the light but cease to flourish when they are in darkness; we too need light and thus fail in the dark. Our darkness, however, is *mâya*, which prevents us from perceiving and growing into our divine nature. Without the celestial light, we end up being unconscious sufferers who wander aimlessly. As the title of one of George's other songs has it, "Unconsciousness Rules."

"Beware Of Darkness" was written for *All Things Must Pass*, near the beginning of George's post-Beatles career. "Brainwashed" was composed thirty years later; and here, at the end, George's preoccupation with the world's darkness remains intact. He judges that we live in a wilderness that exists within "the longest night," within indeed "an eternity of darkness." "Someone," George says, "turned out the spiritual light."

That the light of the world is under a bushel is not just a cynical assessment about the darkness of modern secular times but a critical evaluation of the universal and everlasting human condition as blinded by the darkness of *mâya*. The source of *mâya*—"someone," perhaps the same "someone" who controls and buys and sells people in "While My Guitar Gently Weeps"—is, moreover, clearly not ignorant human beings, who are its victims, but rather some larger, undefined, ill-understood, metaphysical reality, the enemy of God and so the enemy of the rest of us.

One should in this connection credit George for his honesty, for despite his self-conception as an enlightened individual, he freely acknowledges his own ignorance. The "someone" he speaks of in "Brainwashed," the "someone" who has switched off the spiritual light, is unnamed. Notwithstanding, then, his developed theology, there's much George doesn't fathom, and he doesn't hide the fact. He doesn't really know and doesn't attempt to conjecture why the world is the way that it is, why it seems dislocated or—in the words of "Awaiting On You All"—why we are "fallen," or why God so often feels so distant. Light may shine in the darkness, but the darkness has not gone away, and embodied human beings still reside in it.

George knows, however, that, whatever explains *mâya*, life is a God-given educational opportunity, even if all too many fail to take advantage of it. This becomes clear in "Living In The Material World." Sounding a bit like Kafka, George here acknowledges that he really doesn't know what he's doing here. Unlike Kafka, however, he has a hope for something better down the road. He anticipates that he will "see much clearer" after he has lived his life "in the material world." This not only expresses eschatological hope—the afterlife will be a better life—but also interprets life as a learning experience, the benefits of which will manifest themselves in the next world.

George's alienation from the material world, his being in it but not of it,[3] and his hope for a better world after shedding his material body explain why he could seriously regard his many seeming achievements as amounting to nothing much—why, for instance, he comments in *The Beatles' Anthology* that having been a Beatle ultimately isn't that important to him and that even recording his music doesn't really matter. All he truly cares about or wants to care about is the inner knowledge that can free him from the material world. The same attitude lies behind his remark to *Rolling Stone* in 1987 that he is an optimist because, even if the planet were to blow up, the souls that inhabit it would still exist and so would work out their destinies elsewhere. In other words, if one looks at the big picture, even the destruction of the whole world wouldn't matter.

In thinking about this side of George's music, one may quickly become ill at ease. Didn't his belief in *māya*, in the illusory nature of our earthly existence, make George unworldly in a bad sense? Was he not, as the cliché has it, so heavenly minded that he was no earthly good? The notion that those who are otherworldly can be of little help to society is for many of us a common one; it has become the instinctive wisdom. We have all imbibed, directly or indirectly, the Marxist critique of religious zeal, the criticism that hoping for justice and salvation in the world to come discourages us from fighting against injustice and slavery in the here and now.

The problem with this disparagement of much traditional religion or with its application to George is that, while it makes sense in the abstract, it isn't always true to the confusing human facts. The early Christians, for example, were quite otherworldly. They expected Jesus to return soon, and already by the second century their heroes were martyrs, people who had despised this world and found the courage to give up their very lives for hope of heaven. But those same Christians engaged in acts of social beneficence that most others did not. When the plague came to town and the pagan physicians ran to the hills to save their own lives, Christians remained, sharing blankets and water with the sick. Their otherworldliness did not drive out their humanitarian compassion but rather gave them the courage to serve others unselfishly in trying and damaging circumstances.

We perhaps find a similar combination of otherworldliness and authentic social concern in George the Hindu. Although he regarded this world as a chimera, and although he thought the purpose of being here was to get out, he at the very same time showed earnest concern for the well-being of other people, and especially for those in dire suffering. At the instigation of Ravi Shankar, who informed him of the genocide of hundreds of thousands of East Bengalis in Bangladesh (East Pakistan), George used his considerable influence to organize quickly—inside of six weeks from idea to performance—the Concert for Bangladesh, held in Madison Square Garden in 1971. This was before Band Aid, Farm Aid, and Live Aid; in fact, those later charitable concerts owe much of their inspiration to the success of George's concert. George was able to gather a distinguished roster of talent—Eric Clapton, Bob Dylan, Billy Preston, Leon Russell, and Ringo Starr, among others. The event was later released as an album and a film, the proceeds of these designated for displaced refugees. The event marked the beginning of big rock-and-roll personalities exercising the responsibility that should come with being a celebrity in our entertainment-driven society.

The words to the song, "Bangla Desh," which George wrote for the concert, are simple and straightforward, and they reveal a sincere humanitarianism. The lyrics recount, without elaboration, how the songwriter learned of the staggering suffering in Pakistan, and they register his ardent desire to help. There follows a plea to others to join him in offering assistance. He briefly informs them that death and distress have taken hold of Bangladesh, and that although the place is far away, the duty to aid is something he just can't neglect. There is here no sectarian ideology, indeed no theology at all, only the assumption that many human beings will, once they learn of the distress of others, no matter how far away, want to lend a helping hand.

The Concert For Bangladesh was not George's only foray into visible public charity. On June 22, 1990, for instance, he appeared on British television to support the Romanian Angels Appeal which his wife, Olivia, was playing a major role in promoting. This was a charity founded to assist abandoned and institutionalized children in Romania during the tyrannical reign of President Ceausescu and thereafter. George and Olivia appeared on television to promote their cause. George further, in imitation of his altruistic work twenty years earlier, persuaded a number of artists to contribute to an album, among them The Bee Gees, Eric Clapton, Elton John, Van Morrison, Paul Simon, Ringo Starr, The Traveling Wilburys, and Stevie Wonder. Unlike *The Concert For Bangladesh*, this album—*Nobody's Child: Romanian Angel Appeal*—despite some good tracks, sold poorly (and it is hard to find today).

George's humanitarian impulse, his concern for the world and its people, shows up often in his music, not just in "Bangla Desh." "The Day The World Gets 'Round," a passionate protest song of deep disillusionment, holds up, as the (unattained) ideal, helping "each other, hand in hand." Likewise, in "Far East Man," George avows, "I won't let him down," and "got to do what I can." Presumably he is singing about his determination to help impoverished and oppressed peoples half a world away. Less heroically and less politically, we see George's sympathetic heart in "While My Guitar Gently Weeps." This beautiful song, on *The Beatles (The White Album)*, is the antithesis of spiritual triumphalism. George doesn't revel in his own enlightenment; rather, he mourns because love has not conquered all. People—people in general, it seems—have instead been diverted, perverted, and inverted; that is, they have been diverted from the path to God's love and so become perverted, their natures distorted—so much so that they are inverted, by which George means they have everything backward: they neglect what they need and pursue what they need to neglect. The song is plaintive precisely because its composer wishes everyone the best and knows that they are far from it. Their love lies sleeping. George's heart sinks.

George doesn't, in his music, mourn only because other people are in need. He also laments because the material world itself is in need, is in fact in the throes of a disaster. Here George is a typical representative of the sixties generation. In interviews he complained about concrete, nuclear power, the cutting down of forests, the poisoning of air and water, and so on. His music repeatedly makes the same complaint. *Brainwashed*'s "Pisces Fish" gripes about the "smoke signals from the brewery,"[4] and "Tears Of The World"—originally written for *Somewhere In England* but cut—protests that big business is polluting the whole world. "Cockamamie Business" (available on *The Dark Horse Years*) worries about the ozone layer and carps that trees are being cut down in order to serve McDonalds and Burger King (a fact made all the more odious for one who was an ardent vegetarian). George, it doesn't surprise, originally toyed with calling his final album not *Brainwashed* but *Your Planet Is Doomed, Vol. 1*.

The most extensive expression of George's ecological anxiety appears in 1981's "Save The World" on *Somewhere In England*. The song displays a jarring disjunction between lyric and sound. The music itself is jaunty, one reviewer calling it "Pythonesque."[5] But deposited in the middle of this happy musical setting are words that, if read on the page by themselves, are anxious and angry.[6] They condemn those who rape the planet and recount a host of treacherous circumstances that threaten all planetary life. In outer space there are bombs and laser beams, on the earth nuclear waste. Rain forests are becoming paper towels. Birds and wildlife are disappearing. Greenpeace's attempt to save the whales has come up against dog food manufacturers. The ability to make atomic weapons is growing, and dangerous nuclear power plants are spreading. Big business, filled with evil-hearted people who care only about making a quick buck for themselves, is bleeding the earth dry. The song ends with observing that we've already come close to losing the planet—maybe a reference not to ecological disaster but to the cold war in general or to the Cuban missile crisis in particular. George then frets, "We're gonna lose it."

The presupposition of all this ecological doom and gloom is, of course, that the material world is, as the book of Genesis in the Bible has it, a good place—otherwise why mourn its demise? In accord with this, George's music often revels in the natural world. A case in point is the little-known, country-sounding "Sunshine Life For Me (Sail Away Raymond)," which he contributed to Ringo Starr's 1973 self-titled *Ringo*. This is a light song all about getting back to nature. It exults in the thought of leaving the city and returning to the countryside and in the thought of sitting in the sun and in the prospect of sailing on the sea. Its author even confesses, with what one hopes is some hyperbole, that he prefers trees and cornfields to human beings.

All this easy romanticism about nature, which resurfaces in the light and bouncy "Gone Troppo," is not very profound. The depth of reflection is on the same level as, let's say, Three Dog Night's "Out In The Country" and a host of lesser known pop tunes from the 1970s, tunes that reflected the young ecological movement. George's fretting about pollution and other environmental troubles never produced lyrics even remotely as clever or memorable as Neil Young's "After The Gold Rush." But there's no doubting George's sincerity. In real life, he sometimes characterized himself not as a musician but as a gardener, and the pictures of trees and plants on *All Things Must Pass*, *Dark Horse*, *George Harrison*, *Somewhere In England*, and *Brainwashed* constitute a recurrent motif. George was in love with the natural world. And so it is that, in the delightful "Blow Away," which exudes happiness, he communicates his joy by thinking about nature, about the warm wind, the clear bright sky, and rainbows. It is the same in "Mystical

One," where, in reaching for a way to express his joy, George ends up saying that he is "happier than a willow tree." This peculiar comparison, whatever else it may convey, clearly stems from George's personal sense of delight in the natural world.

All this leads to a vexing question. How do we harmonize George's relentlessly otherworldly attitude, his repeated conviction that he has no care for what he calls the "lower world" (in "That Which I Have Lost"), with his obvious joy in and care for the material world and his fellow human beings? One might suppose that there is a contradiction here and let it go at that. On the one hand, George was a religious Hindu, and Hinduism instructs its adherents about *mâya* and about the passing nature of the material world. On the other hand, George was also a product of the idealism of the 1960s and the burgeoning ecological movement. He came of age when many young people were chanting "Make love, not war," when John Lennon was singing "Give peace a chance," when car bumpers commanded us to "Save the Whales," and when so many naïvely thought that they could insist upon a better way and profoundly alter the course of history. Dylan spoke for them when he sang, "the times they are a-changin'."

George, there is no doubt, imbibed in large measure the dreamy idealism of his generation. Like his good friend, Derek Taylor (press officer for Apple), he at one time really believed that, with the advent of his revolutionary generation, the world was about to become "a much, much nicer place" than heretofore.[7] And until the end George in some ways sounded like a sixties radical. He often railed against the military and war—not this or that war, but all war, war in general, as if goodhearted people could do without it if they just tried hard enough—and he never lost his sixties disrespect, already documented in "Piggies" on *The Beatles (The White Album)*, for big business and big greed. "Brainwashed" grumbles about international capitalism in the form of the Nikkei (Japan's stock exchange), the Dow Jones, the FTSE (the share index of the hundred largest companies on the London Stock Exchange), and the Nasdaq (the U.S. electronic stock exchange); and it shuns Brussels, Bonn, Washington, and London, cities representing the world's most powerful economic and political capitals.

George goes on in "Brainwashed" to plead with God to lead the world out of the mess it's got itself into. Refusing to "accept defeat," he wistfully sings, "If we can only stop the rot." Here some sort of collectivist vision or hope seems to assert itself. George desperately wants a different world, one without the evils of big business, big polluters, and big war mongers. His voice is that of a sixties radical who has not, despite everything, been able to let go completely of the old utopian vision. The same voice also still appears to speak in "Far East Man," where George professes that "a heaven's in sight." Notwithstanding the failure of his revolutionary times, some part of him still holds a melioristic hope, a hope that people might be able to make the world a truly better place. One recalls that another Beatle, Ringo Starr, was still singing, in 2003, about "peace and love" and "harmony" and asking, "How hard can it be?" ("Eye To Eye" on *Ringo Rama*).

But there is much more to say than this. It is not enough to suppose that George's musical musings about the material world are just the contradictory upshots of his indoctrination into the idealistic dreams of the 1960s and his simultaneous embracing of a philosophical Hinduism. For the seeming paradox in his ideology, his studied indifference toward the material world on the one hand and his passionate love and hope for it and its people on the other hand, belong precisely to his adopted Hinduism. That is, George inherited the tension from the modern Indian religious tradition, which is very far from promoting religious escapism or an ethical nihilism. He was greatly indebted to nineteenth- and twentieth-century Hindu thinkers such as Rajnarain Bose, who was one of the so-called Brahmo leaders. They were modern Hindus of strong social conscience who, influenced by Christianity, argued against navel-gazing and for honoring one's fellow human beings.

The Maharishi reportedly told the Beatles in 1967: "You have created a magic air through your names. You have now got to use that magic influence on the generation who look up to you. You have a big responsibility." The Beatles supposedly accepted his challenge. Whether that is the truth or not, George himself, notwithstanding his world-denying ideology, always felt that his religion itself instilled in him a responsibility for caring for the material world and its people. The *Bhagavad-Gita* already enjoins its readers to work for "the maintenance of the world" (3:20), and this imperative has been taken to mean that, "if the world is not to sink into a condition of physical misery and moral degradation, if the common life is to be decent and dignified, religious ethics must control social action."[8] In line with this, George sang, in "Living In The Material World," that, before leaving this place, he had much work to do, and that he had to get a message out. George is to live his life, it seems, partly on behalf of others. Indeed, maybe it is not an exaggeration to say that, at times, George came close to having a sort of prophetic self-conception, that he was a man who felt an overwhelming need to share with others his important discoveries. As he sang in "Poor Little Girl," "There's a need and desire . . . to express what's inside of me." In any case, his need to protest, to speak out and make himself be heard, was not just a countercultural leftover from sixties radicalism. It likewise belonged to his religion.

If George's humanitarian impulse is consistent with his Hindu religiosity, it is not really otherwise with his ecological orientation. This is because, even though the material world is, for him, illusory, is *mâya*, is a veil over the face of God, it is nonetheless a divine manifestation and so can serve to manifest the Deity. This is why George so often sings about finding God in the natural world, which he calls, in "Dear One," "creation," and likewise why, in "Here Comes The Moon," which is about a sunset in Hawaii, he interprets the natural world as "God's gift." It is clear from George's music that God is not just the creator but is equally the sustainer of this material world. "Life Itself" tells us that God sends the rain and brings the sun. Here, life-giving light and water from heaven are not just natural phenomena; their ultimate explanation is God's goodness. This is perhaps why, in "This Is Love," the sun not only "melts the chill from our lives" but functions to help us recall what we are here for, which for George must mean God-consciousness. George can even assert, in "Fish On The Sand," that God is in the sun and in the moon. Although he doesn't elaborate, we know from "Sat Singing," which we have already considered at some length in an earlier chapter, that at least the sun was once an integral part of one of George's most profound religious experiences. And in this song George seems to find God both "deep within himself" and in the "external world." The kingdom of God is, to recall George's old Beatles' song, both "within you and without you."

If George cannot be criticized for being so otherworldly as to be no earthly good, it remains true that the emphasis in his music is upon the individual and not society, and further that his hopes lie ultimately not in this material world but in some transcendent realm. Concerning this material world and its problems, he has wishes but no answers. He says this plainly enough in "Stuck Inside A Cloud," where he tells us that he wishes he had "the answer" or "the cure," but confides that he doesn't. His tone here conveys nothing of his one-time sixties optimism but instead expresses some world weariness and social cynicism. Although his public actions throughout his life indicate that he believed politics should be pursued to amend the evils of modern society (in the 1992 U.K. elections he made known his support for The Natural Law Party, TM's political wing), sad experience had taught him that the pursuit was probably vain, an ideal never to be even remotely approached, and so political parties and movements and solutions are mostly irrelevant in George's musical message. His gospel is rather, in the last analysis, that all we can do is improve ourselves, that our best contribution to the world is bettering ourselves. He did not have faith that the human condition could really be enhanced by public means. Instead he believed in changing human hearts through a religious awakening. In the end, the massive problems of society leave George flummoxed. The only answers he has are religious, and they are for the individual. In one of his last interviews, George said that he had no worries whatever about his place in creation, but he thought the world's environment doomed. One may compare this to the lyrics of "Headed For The Light," where George, despite feeling great changes within himself, looks around and sees "nothing new." The world goes on as ever.

The most blatant illustration of George's resignation regarding the world at large is "Save The World." This strange song is, as we have seen, a conventional litany of the world's woes. It bewails the expansion of the weapons of war, the buildup of nuclear waste, the devastation of the world's wildlife, and so forth. George wants the madness to stop, because future generations will need the world, too. He recognizes, however, that some evil-hearted people, although few in number, have enough power to turn the earth into a "hell"; and they are trying to do this because it brings them personal profit for the present. But having made this complaint, George abruptly changes gears. Out of the blue, in a verbal transition as striking as the discord between the irate words and the jaunty, cheery tune, George announces that he is going to end on "a happy note." That note is this: what counts is the fundamental fact that "God lives in your hearts."

One is initially baffled by this curious disjunction, by the unexpected transition from one subject to another apparently unrelated. At first one tries to find some train of thought, some logical connection between saving the world and God's living in our hearts. Perhaps George is exhorting us to imagine that, if enough of us come to recognize the God who lives in our hearts, then we will be changed, and then we can perhaps save the world after all. But this is to misread what happens in the song at this point. George makes the unexpected move from enumeration of worldwide woe to the wonderful news that God lives within our hearts because he has given up on the former and can find refuge only in the latter. The sudden movement from the perils devouring the world to personal piety is really a sign of surrender, the end of all political idealism. As he puts it simply on *Gone Troppo*, "That's The Way It Goes." George doesn't believe that we should not care for the material world—he profoundly mourns its peril and its people's miseries—but he does know that he can't fix things, and that maybe nobody can fix things. So if he is not to be passive, if he is to do something useful, maybe the most useful thing left is to fix himself, or rather to find the God within who can fix him. As he says in "Cockamamie Business," "You do what you can, you can't do much more than that." In the end, then, George is optimistic about God but pessimistic about life in the material world, the world which he dearly loves in so many ways.

Notes

1. Paramahansa Yogananda, *Autobiography of a Yogi* (Los Angeles: Self-Realization Fellowship, 1990), 310.

2. Available online at: www.krishna.org/Articles/2000/08/00066.html.

3. In his 1974 Los Angeles Press Conference George quoted the language of the Bible: "to be in the world but not of the world." He introduced this with: "as they say."

4. Given that these works are followed by a reference to the appointment of the latest Pope, one assumes George is at the same time alluding to the ritual of smoke coming from the chimney of the Sistine Chapel during a

papal conclave. Black smoke means a vote has been inconclusive. White smoke means the cardinals have reached a decision.

5. Simon Leng, *The Music of George Harrison: While My Guitar Gently Weeps* (London: Fire Fly, 2003), 171–72.

6. In his *Creem* interview (December 1987, January 1988), he cryptically commented that "Save The World" is "serious and funny at the same time."

7. Taken from a 1999 interview with Taylor, available at: http://21stcentury radio.com/NP-8-25-99.1.html.; accessed 9/12/05.

8. Sarvepalli Radhakrishnan and Charles A. Moore, *A Sourcebook in Indian Philosophy* (Princeton: Princeton University Press, 1957), 114.

The Art of Dying

DEATH AND REINCARNATION

To be born is like being hanged: it's only a matter of time before we're done. We're all condemned to die. But being alive is in and of itself a positive thing, and we typically dread the inevitable. Our dread has deep biological roots. Even spiders exhibit the will to live, which is why they flee from us when we attempt to extinguish them. Eventually, to be sure, when we become sufficiently elderly and infirm or if, before that, our psychological or physical pain has become overwhelming, we may sadly resign ourselves to death. Otherwise, however, we desperately wish to go on living. This is why, notwithstanding the numerous agonies that life inflicts upon us, few ever seriously attempt suicide. Most of us feel most of the time that inexorable doom is unwelcome, maybe even the most terrible thing of all. Dying appears to cancel everything that has gone before it and so seemingly destroys the meaning of our lives. We accordingly try to keep ourselves busy, that our minds might attend to something other than our upcoming erasure. Filling our lives with this task and that amusement, we anxiously push our dismal apprehension of death's inevitability away from our conscious minds. We may even fantasize about extending our material lives, perhaps through exercising more or eating better or being the beneficiaries of some new scientific breakthrough. In any event, death is our enemy. A recent survey of Britons by *New Scientist* found 67 percent of respondents absolutely petrified by the prospect of meeting the Grim Reaper.

George's lyrics confront us with something completely different. George doesn't nervously run from the subject of death, which he instead ponders frequently in his music. Nor, when he addresses this topic, does it terrify him. Unlike John Fogerty on Creedence Clearwater Revival's "Walk On The Water," George never says, "I don't want to go; I don't want to go; no, no, no, no, I don't want to go." On the contrary, George wants to go. He welcomes death. He typically perceives the end of life as a dramatic opportunity, as a door that can, if one is rightly prepared, open wide onto another and better world and beckon us enter.

Some idea of George's preoccupation with death and its aftermath—not exactly standard fare for most pop artists—can be gained from glancing through the following list of Harrisongs:

- "Within You Without You" warns that some "never glimpse the truth" before it's "too late," that is, before they "pass away."
- "All Things Must Pass" is a touching reflection on the transience of all things, including human love and life.
- "Art Of Dying" is, as we shall see, an extended meditation on the importance of preparing for death.
- "Give Me Love" prays that the singer may be kept "free from birth," that is, avoid returning to this world after leaving it.
- "Living In The Material World" refers to George seeing "much clearer" after he leaves this world.
- "The Lord Loves The One (That Loves The Lord)" asks, "Who will stand and who will fall?" when death finally comes.
- "The Answer's At The End" construes life as a great question that will only be answered when it is over.

THE LOVE THERE THAT'S SLEEPING

- "Grey Cloud Lies" recalls an occasion when the singer contemplated suicide.
- "Crackerbox Palace" says that those who live differently than the majority may find themselves deported, which for George must mean being unshackled from the karma that keeps returning us, upon death, to the material world.
- "Life Itself" records George's promise that he would die for God's sake; it then addresses God as "the light in death" that George will see when he's done with this life.
- "All Those Years Ago" imagines the afterlife as a place of freedom and light.
- "That Which I Have Lost" has it that "mortality" is part of the "lower world" and teaches that desire, busyness, and fear of death bar one from getting back to the "higher world."
- "Writing's On The Wall" contemplates the folly of holding on to material things even as death draws nearer day by day.
- "Circles" has as its subject reincarnation; George wishes to break out of the cycle of death and rebirth, to prevent his soul from returning to a body in this world.
- "That's What It Takes" is about the singer getting closer to "that open door," that is, to death, and he resolves to have "what it takes" in order to enter the antimaterial heavenly world.
- "Headed For The Light" announces that George is moving toward God, whom he will find fully in death.
- "Pisces Fish" expresses the singer's longing to get off "of this big wheel," which means he wants to escape the cycle of rebirth; the song also has George hoping to find an "unbounded ocean of bliss" in the next world.
- "Looking For My Life" is George's musical reflection upon his close encounter with death at the hands of a madman in 1999.

The length of this list, which could be enlarged, is instructive. Clearly George thought a great deal about death and the afterlife.

If one asks why this should be so, why George was so interested in contemplating mortality, in rehearsing his own death, and in dreaming about the afterlife, the answer is not that he was compelled to do so by serious illness or accident. Although "Grey Cloud Lies" looks back on a depression that led George to entertain killing himself, and while "Looking For My Life" was occasioned by a near-fatal stabbing, these songs are exceptional. The remainder of George's musical reflections on death did not derive from situations where death seemed at hand.

In trying to understand George's obvious fixation, maybe it's not out of place to observe that death is often an obsession of the young. Sometime after puberty, when childhood is gone, people may seriously confront their own transience for the first time, and this can lead to a personal crisis. Surely many teenagers undergo a religious conversion or renewal precisely because it helps them to cope with their newfound consciousness of the inevitable. And perhaps this partly explains why George was already singing about death when he was in his twenties, when death was likely decades away; and perhaps his embracing of Hinduism was a way of resolving his youthful anxiety.

Whatever the merit of such speculation may be, it is worth observing that, in writing songs about death, George did have some obvious forerunners. For one thing, he was a Beatle, and The Beatles had not completely ignored human mortality. They briefly broached the subject in two of their finest productions. McCartney's "Eleanor Rigby" is a sober and sad meditation upon loneliness, and it focuses upon the funeral of a seemingly meaningless life just ended. Similarly, Lennon's "In My Life" reflects upon the dead as well as the living, upon people who have gone before.

Much more importantly, George was throughout his life greatly enamored of Bob Dylan's music, in which death is a recurrent theme. Dylan's first album, *Bob Dylan* (1963), features three songs—all covers—whose main subject is death: "In My Time Of Dyin'," "Fixin' To Die Blues," and "See That My Grave's Kept Clean." In addition, two other songs on that album refer to death—"Man Of Constant Sorrow" and "Highway 51 Blues." Dylan's later work offers more of the same. "Tombstone Blues" appears on *Highway 51 Revisited* (1965), "Knockin' On Heaven's Door" on *Pat Garrett And Billy The Kid* (1973), and "Silvio"—the refrain of which includes: "I gotta go, find out something only dead men know"—on *Down In The Grove* (1988). One could cite literally dozens of relevant songs from the Dylan canon. So given Dylan's enormous influence upon George, we can at least say that the former supplied the latter with prominent precedent for using popular music as a means for sharing thoughts about death.

What really interests us, however, are not the biographical circumstances that may have contributed to George's feeling free to share his convictions about death but rather what precisely he had to say about it. And here again we encounter his thoroughly Hindu outlook.

It is possible to view death, as do many modern people, as our natural and necessary conclusion, as nature's inevitable means of making room for new generations; and one can, if so inclined, work up the courage to resign oneself to oblivious extinction. If it is the case that we altogether cease to exist, so that the afterlife's like a dreamless sleep from which we never awake, then, as Socrates asked, what is there to fear?

George will have none of this. He firmly believes instead in an eternal "soul" (he uses the word in its proper metaphysical sense in both "Circles" and "Pisces Fish"); and the soul's continued existence after this life is central to all of his theological reflections. Death is not extermination but passage to another life. The only question is whether one's next life will be in this "lower" material world—reincarnation—or in some "higher" and better world. It is the latter that George ardently desires, the former that he fervently wishes to avoid.

The prospect of reincarnation and its undesirable nature appear in a number of songs. The most blatant example is "Circles," on *Gone Troppo*. Here the singer says straight out: "the soul reincarnates." (Despite the importance of this concept for his worldview, this is the only time George, anywhere in his lyrics, uses the verb, "reincarnate." The noun, "reincarnation," never shows up.) "Circles" speaks of "each birth," which occurs when a "soul takes on a body." What George means is that we are not born once; each of us rather has multiple births. We have entered this material world many times before and will enter it many times again. Death and life are for us cyclical: "the show goes round and round in circles."

Although this is a form of immortality, it is not what George desires. As he says in "Pisces Fish," he ardently longs "to get off of this big wheel," or as he prays in "Give Me Love," he wants to be "free from birth." How does this happen? One gets off the big wheel and avoids rebirth, according to "Circles," when "up" and "down" are the same, or when "gain" and "loss" are equal; then the circle is broken. The words are cryptic and require some explanation. They presuppose the Hindu doctrine of *mâya*, according to which the material world is a grand illusion. All the multiplicity and diversity are in truth manifestations of the one hidden and divine reality. Despite appearances, then, all is one. So the individual who recognizes the illusory nature of this world, who perceives the unity behind all the diversity, and who understands that *mâya* is a divine mask realizes that opposites are not opposites. To understand that up is down and that gain is loss is to be enlightened; it is to overcome "limitation"—the word George uses in "That Which I Have Lost"—and to be on one's way to escaping from the material world.

Other songs convey as well that enlightenment overcomes the illusion of duality. In "Blow Away," George at one point speaks of a moment in which his head was filled with light. He attaches to the experience the laconic phrase, "instant amnesia." One assumes that the two words—which Ringo later turned into the title of a fine rocker for *Ringo Rama*—are a rewrite of Lennon's famous "Instant Karma" (for which George played the guitar). In George's song, "instant amnesia" is a way of conveying that, in or through a recent religious experience, he has been enabled to leave behind his past errors and their negative karma. There then follows the cryptic phrase, "yang to the yin." In Chinese philosophy, the yin and yang represent all the opposites in the universe, opposites that, in a never ending cycle, constantly bring each other into being. In George's religious experience, however, the eternal recurrence, the never ending production of opposites, has revealed itself as illusory. His ecstatic enlightenment has brought or confirmed the realization that all is one.

Equally instructive in this connection is "Dream Away." This charming song contains a whole series of mysterious antitheses. There is sunshine at midnight, thunder that is silent, a day that is black, a waking that is sleeping, and a discovery that finds nothing; and the song approaches its end by juxtaposing "in" with "out," "hot" with "cold," "up" with "down," and "young" with "old." Amid all this is the repeated line, "Only a dream away." Once again George is telling us cryptically about *mâya*. The world is a dream, filled with what appear to be fundamental antitheses. But if one can wake up from the dream, can get past the illusory opposites, can perceive that up is truly down and that young is truly old, then one can begin to escape the forces that have kept us reincarnating again and again. The world and its characteristic opposites are "only a dream." Waking from that dream brings knowledge and freedom.

Another way of expressing this conviction occurs in "Hear Me Lord," on *All Things Must Pass*. Instead of saying clearly that all is one, George rather tells us that God is "in" every place—"out and in," "above and below," "to the left and the right," and "at both ends of the road." This confession of God's ubiquity, of the divine presence in all opposites, introduces a prayer that the singer may rise a little "higher," by which he means: get closer to God. He can do this by burning out his "desire." Here it is rejection of attachment to the material world that enables one to rise above every seeming antithesis and to approach the God who relativizes all opposites by being in all of them.

George reportedly once said to a friend: "We are just water and molecules here on a visit." It would have been more accurate had George said that we are just water and molecules that *should* be only on a visit. The problem is that, instead of staying for a brief time, we constantly keep returning to this vale of tears, as though the material world were our proper home, which it is not. Because of attachment to the illusory world of opposites, we are, instead of saying good-bye, constantly saying hello. We thus live through "a million years of crying" ("Art Of Dying"), live again and again through "a thousand centuries" ("Only A Dream Away"). George cares about death because he cares about what comes after death. He doesn't want more of the same but more of God. "The whole point to being here," then, "is to figure a way to get out."[1]

Given that death is inevitable and that it leads either to a higher world or to reincarnation in the material world, it is foolish to ignore the crossroads ahead. If "The Answer's At The End," as George tells us on *Extra Texture: Read All About It*, then it should be incumbent upon us to contemplate and prepare for that end. We should not just live in the here and now; we should instead contemplate the future that is coming toward us and do our best to take advantage of it and of the opportunity it holds. It is true that, on *Living In The Material World*, George implores us to "Be Here Now," and this song must be understood as an endorsement of the once well-known book, *Be Here Now* (1971), written by Ram Das. (Ram Das is the Hindu name for Dr. Richard Alpert, a one-time Harvard psychologist who, like Timothy

Leary, was dismissed for his controversial work with LSD.) Das's *Be Here Now* is a popular introduction to Hindu spirituality. It emphasizes that the future has not yet come and so is unknown, and that the past has gone and can never be again, so all we have is the present. Real life, then, can only be lived right now. George, who must have written the song shortly after reading the book, seconds all this by borrowing the title of the latter and bestowing it upon the former.

Although the lesson of "Be Here Now" shows up again in "Flying Hour" (a song withdrawn from *Somewhere In England*), it is hardly the typical George, who is not only given to dwelling sometimes nostalgically upon the past (as in "All Those Years Ago" and "When We Was Fab") but who encourages all of us to ponder our inescapable end and so imagine the future. In fact, one of George's criticisms of human beings is that we often live only in the present. Shunning uncomfortable thoughts, we typically live in denial of death. Suppressing our fears, we live as though we will always be here, and as though the material things that we long to acquire and our mindless recreations—George particularly skewers nightlife and partying—are worthwhile. As "Writing On The Wall" observes, we senselessly latch onto material possessions even as death approaches to take possession of us.

All of us. The disease that leads to death, George stresses, spares no one. "The Lord Loves The One (That Loves The Lord)" remarks that even the rich and famous, who have what the rest of us irrationally imagine we want, "don't escape old age creeping, through their bodies, like a rot." This is, of course, obvious; it almost seems silly to say it. And yet, in this material world, where the "Unconsciousness Rules," we are all "Brainwashed." Instead of acknowledging what cannot be doubted, that "All Things Must Pass," we pretend otherwise. We all know that death is like taxes and that we can't take anything with us, but George observes that this makes no difference. We remain victims of *māya*. As it says in the Katha Upanishad: "Intoxicated, deluded by the glamour of riches, the childish do not see that they must pass away. They think, 'This is the world and there is no other.'"

Human folly in this matter is all the more egregious because no one knows when death will come. The ancient rabbis taught: Repent a day before your death. The meaning of course is that, since we never know when the angel of death may suddenly appear, we should repent

THE LOVE THERE THAT'S SLEEPING

every day. George similarly knows that death is an ever-present possibility, that life can be cut short at any moment. So we need to begin to practice the "Art Of Dying" now. But, as "That Which I Have Lost" has it, we are "too busy," so that we ensure our unfortunate return to this "lower world." In "Pisces Fish," George asks us whether we will have time to sort everything out. Implied is a word of warning: begin today, because tomorrow may be too late. Likewise, in "Within You Without You," George admonishes us that, unless we seek "the truth" now, we may find that the time is "far too late," that is, death, which has its own schedule, will terminate our opportunities.

But what, we must now ask, does George have to say about death itself? Death is, proverbially, thanks to Shakespeare, "the undiscover'd country from whose bourn no traveler returns." Unless one believes in mediums, it is not clear that those who have gone before us have crossed back over the river of death to give us the details of their discoveries. For George, however, death is not the great unknown. He rather has a whole set of convictions about what happens to us when we die.

For one thing, George believes that, at death, there is a sort of judgment (although he himself never uses that word). In "The Lord Loves The One (That Loves The Lord)," he ridicules the world's leaders. He tells us that they act "like big girls" and fail to think about God. But the joke is on them. For when they die, George knowingly asks, "Who will stand, and who will fall?" There are, obviously, two possible outcomes, and they are antithetical—standing and falling. Further, some of those who have thought they will stand instead will fall. By this George doesn't mean that the living will evaluate a life just completed, with perhaps surprising results. His idea is not that of the old proverb, "Call no one blessed until he dies," which means that an individual's story is like a novel: we can't assess the whole without knowing the ending. George is nowhere concerned with what others think of us when we die, nor with the meaning of our lives within history. The judgment that we face at death, and what matters to George, is not the verdict rendered by other people but the ruling of the cosmic law of karma and the God who stands beyond history.

What happens to us at death is the upshot of our words and deeds. These are, according to "Rising Sun," kept in some sort of internal "file," both "the good and the bad." Using another metaphor, George sings in "Simply Shady" that life is like a pebble thrown into the ocean. When the pebble enters, it creates waves that spread out in all directions. So, too, is it with our lives. Our actions send out waves of influence. Moreover, instead of dissipating, they meet up with us later on, especially at death. As George puts it, our actions "reach from here to there," and our "influence in motion" will rebound and come back toward us. Our deeds do not leave us or forsake us, and we can never repudiate them. They will go with us to the grave. And when George sings, "the action that I've started, sometime I'll have to face," he is anticipating his death and its attendant judgment. What we have done clings to us, and if our karma is negative, it will draw us back into this world.[2]

In this connection it may be appropriate to note that George's music has no place for the concept of hell. For him, the stark alternative at death is not heaven versus hell but liberation versus reincarnation. It's true that George does sometimes use the word, "hell," but (like so many from the past two centuries) he always employs it as a sort of metaphor. In "Far Eastern Man," for instance, he remarks that life can be "hellish at times"; and in "Save The World," he worries that modern inventions and greed are going to reduce this planet to "hell." But George never warns us that death might issue in some sort of eternal torment. Apparently, the retributive torture chamber of much of his native Christian tradition was one of the things George left behind when he adopted his brand of Hinduism.

Although no one is bound for hell, there is clearly some sort of heaven, or rather better planes of existence and lastly *moksha*, or final liberation and union with God. If people properly prepare themselves for death, so that their karma doesn't fasten them to this material world, they can stop going in circles and returning here and instead move on to a celestial existence. What sort of place or existence will they then find themselves in? Here George is appropriately modest. Just as he suggests no theory to explain the origin of death—he doesn't, for example, say that the wages of sin is death—so too he offers us no map of the heavenly planes, no blueprint of the world to come. Yet of one thing he is convinced, and this is that the higher world is a world of light.

This is striking because death, the great unknown, has frequently been represented as darkness, as in the *Epic of Gilgamesh*—it's the house "bereft of light"—or in the *Iliad*—"death is near, and black"—or in

Tennyson—"Twilight and evening bell, and after that the dark." Job put it most memorably: "Are not the days of my life few? Let me alone, that I may find a little comfort before I go whence I shall not return, to the land of gloom and deep darkness, the land of gloom and chaos where light is as darkness." Death is, to use an old phrase, a "leap into the dark."

For George, however, the happier world beyond death is light. In "Headed For The Light," which George wrote for The Traveling Wilburys, he sings that he sees "the sun ahead." He is referring to what he will find in his own death, which he likens to the brightest object in our experience. If there is any doubt as to the meaning, it is dispelled by "Life Itself," where George calls God the "light in death." And then there is "All Those Years Ago," where George expresses his belief that John Lennon, recently murdered, is now in "the world of light."

What is perhaps most remarkable about these references to the light is how brimming with confidence, even enthusiasm, they are. George seems persuaded that all is well with his soul, so that he too is destined, like his friend John, for "the world of light." The prospect indeed fills him with delight. The rocking "Headed For The Light" is happy and upbeat. It is "Here Comes The Sun" moved to the afterlife. The singer sounds exultant as he bids farewell to his past and observes that all his dreams are "coming true." He indeed goes on to declare that "nothing [is] in the way to stop me heading for the light." George, so far from running away from death, is running toward it. His is the view of Paramahansa Yogananda: "The tragedy of death is unreal; those who shudder at it are like an ignorant actor who dies of fright on the stage when nothing more has been fired at him than a blank cartridge."[3]

It's the same in "Life Itself," even if the music is more subdued. The touching ballad is confident. George professes that, when he dies, he will encounter God, and he identifies this God with "the breath of life itself." How can death really be death if the Life-giver is waiting on the other side? George, moreover, believes that this Life-giver he will meet is also "love," "the truth," and "all that is real." Even more, this God is George's dear friend. Sounding like a child, the singer addresses the Supreme Being directly: "You are my friend, and when life's through, you are the light in death itself." These touching words, and the depth of feeling in the singer's voice, clearly reflect a trusting familiarity that has cast out all fear. As death will bring George nearer to his divine friend, the eventuality cannot be dreaded but only hoped for. It accords with this that, in "Pisces Fish," George sings of swimming until he finds the waters that are "one unbounded ocean of bliss."[4] That is what it will be like to meet God.

It's telling that, when George thinks of who will be waiting for him on the other side, he apparently thinks of God alone, not of other human beings. The usual modern accounts of deathbed visions and of near-death experiences are full of deceased friends and relatives. It's probably safe to generalize that when people think of the afterlife, they typically think of it in social terms, as a reunion with loved ones who have gone before. As the nineteenth-century Christian hymn has it, "In the sweet by-and-by, we shall meet on that beautiful shore." Or, as Dylan sings in "Man Of Constant Sorrow," "I'll see you on God's golden shore." Here heaven means meeting others once again. In Harrisongs, however, it's just George and God. The intensity of his feelings for the Deity displaces all thought of meeting up again with others. George seemingly longs to see only God, who is, in the words of "When We Was Fab," his whole "world" and his "only love." In one song he prays to God, "I Live For You." He could equally have sung, "I Die For You."

One may, at this point, want to ask, How can George presume to instruct us about death before he has experienced it? How can he pretend to know anything before the fact of his own demise? The answer, of course, is that he believes what he believes because he has accepted the teachings of his religious tradition. His acceptance of karma and reincarnation, and his idea of a spiritual world of light and bliss, are adopted from his Hindu teachers. For instance, one of the most important books in George's life was Paramahansa Yogananda's *Autobiography of a Yogi* (portions of which he read to his mother on her deathbed). Chapter 30 is entitled, "The Law of Miracles," and it is full of propositions about light. Yogananda teaches that, of all natural manifestations, light is "the freest from material dependence," that "Einstein banished from the universe every fixed reality except that of light," that the essence of atoms is light, that the masters who have done miracles have done so by manipulating light rays, that light is the immaterial medium of all divine manifestations, and that the universe is "essentially" an "undifferentiated mess of light."[5]

Furthermore, Yogananda addresses God in a prayer as "Divine Light" and recounts his own mystical visions of supernatural lights. Clearly George's infatuation with light and his associations of it with the Divinity have their parallels in Yogananda. Yogananda's ideas in turn are representative of the broader Hindu tradition. The *Kaivalya Upanishad*, for example, says that the Supreme Lord is "fire" and "self-illumined" and "beyond all darkness," and the *Mundaka Upanishad* calls Brahman the "light of all lights."

Yet it would be a mistake to say no more than that George's beliefs are the upshot of what he has read or been taught, for his conception of the afterlife is also, in some important ways, an extrapolation from or intensification of his own present experience. The future, that is, holds in full what George has in part already known. Although "Pisces Fish" conceives of our heavenly destination as a boundless sea of delight, the song also says that this spiritual reality even now flows through all of us. Perception of this fact may be easily missed, but the ocean is nonetheless there. The implication is that the bliss of encounter with the divine can be known to human experience even before death.

That this is the case is crystal clear from what George has to say about light. If the higher world which we can enter at death is full of divine radiance, it is also possible to experience the transcendent light in the here and now. It's not just that the sun and moon, which reflect the glory of their Creator, show themselves to us regularly—everyday facts that George doesn't take for granted but intensely celebrates ("Here Comes The Sun," "Here Comes The Moon," etc.). It's also the case that, in the midst of this material world, we have access to "spiritual light" ("Brainwashed"). When George calls God "The Light That Has Lighted The World," he is referring to this world, and not just to its heavenly orbs. God is already, in the present, our "guiding light" ("Your Love Is Forever"). Even now the Supreme Being enlightens us ("That Which I Have Lost").

This means not only that we can have genuine knowledge and understanding of the Divinity (as in "The Inner Light" and "Deep Blue") but also that, while yet in our material bodies, we can have literal visions of the divine light (as maybe "Blow Away" recounts). George is thinking of both things—visions and knowledge—when, in "Give Me Love," he prays to God, "give me light." Thus the various sorts of lights that he knows in this world—the lights in the sky, the light of understanding, and the light of mystical experience—are the presence of the transcendent divinity in the midst of this mundane world. From one point of view, then, they are the heavenly future coming into the present. The higher world will be an intensification and perfecting of George's encounters with the divine light while living in the material world. In this way, religious doctrine, including teaching about the world to come, is anchored in present experience.

Most of what George has to say about death comes to expression in "The Art Of Dying," which may have been written as early as 1966 (when he was only twenty-two or twenty-three years old), although it did not appear until *All Things Must Pass* (1970). Fortunately, George himself supplies a fairly lengthy analysis of the lyrics in *I, Me, Mine*.[6]

The first thing that strikes one about the song is the arresting title. We usually think of an art as a skill acquired by experience or study, as something at which one has to work. But what can it mean to work at death? How could we ever fail at it? Everyone dies. Even plants have what it takes to die. Giving up the ghost is not the outcome of study but happens to all living things, no matter what. Further, how could it ever be practiced? We cannot die once and then try again if it somehow goes badly. Surely dying is anything but an art.

And yet George invites us to practice the art of dying. What does he mean? One is reminded of the Greek philosopher Plato, who attributed to his teacher, Socrates, the belief that to study philosophy is to learn how to die, so that authentic philosophers "are always engaged in the practice of dying." For Plato, philosophy turns the mind away from the material world of the senses to the more real but unseen realities that can only be perceived and understood with the mind's eye; and turning away from the visible world to contemplation of the invisible world is preparation for death, which shuttles us from the one world to the other. The upshot, for the authentic philosopher, is that death is not feared but embraced.

George is not so different in all this from Plato. To practice the art of dying is to learn that the material world is not reality. It is to focus one's attention on the invisible ocean of bliss that flows through all things, the ocean that is our ultimate destiny. One turns the act of dying into an art by ever enlarging one's understanding and experience of the true nature of things. This means seeing through *māya*. It means seeking enlightenment. It means abandoning the desires that keep one attached to this material world. Those who successfully accomplish those things will find that the sting of death is drawn and that they "can consciously leave the body at death, as opposed to falling down dying without knowing what's going on."[7]

Turning from the title to the opening stanza, its six lines, introduced by urgent and haunting guitar licks (presumably Clapton's), do several things. They start with the obvious, that "all of us" will someday "leave here," and that nothing can prevent this from happening. So George begins with the universality of death. The upshot is that his topic inevitably concerns each of us. How can we not be interested? Next, George declares that nothing he has attempted in this life can compare with the art of dying. By this he means that the most important thing in life is the leaving of it. Nothing matters more. This is, of course, because death is not an end but a beginning, the start of a new existence, good or bad. Finally, George concludes the first stanza by asking, "Do you believe me?" The singer knows that what he is saying—death is more important than life—will seem counterintuitive, even wildly implausible to many. He fully appreciates that listeners may not credit his claim. Instead of preaching down to them, he asks a question that serves as an invitation to reflection. He is gently prodding us to think along with him.

In the second stanza, George reiterates that death will take us all, but he now conceptualizes the event as the fading of hope: when death shows itself, it will cancel all our dreams and well-laid plans. The result will be "an awful pain." Dying will awaken us to the realization that what we have valued is not of enduring value. Yet recognition that our aspirations and achievements cannot help us at the end will not in the end help us. For although we may then desperately begin to look "for the truth among the lying," it will be too late, because we have not heretofore practiced the art of dying. We will be unprepared.

The last stanza opens by informing listeners that if they want "it"—presumably the truth learned by practicing the art of dying—then they need to "find it." This is George's version of the Bible's "seek and ye shall find." Without effort, there can be no result. That is straightforward enough: it's not easy to leave this world rightly. But George adds a riddle

The Art of Dying

for us here. He goes on to say that, once we "have it," we won't "need" it. The cryptic and perhaps humorous remark is likely a way of saying that, once an individual has mastered the art of dying, he or she will go on to the higher world and so will no longer have to practice that art. Once we perfect the art, we will no longer need it.

The closing lines are, by contrast, unambiguous. George discloses that "most of us" will come back "here." This is an assertion that reincarnation is the common human predicament. His brief explanation is that our "desire" keeps returning us to this inferior material world. Happily, however, we also all have within us a legitimate desire—to be "a perfect entity." So although reincarnation entails that we live "through a million years of crying," George leaves us with the impression that the inborn desire for perfection in a better world will, eventually, move us to douse our other desires and enable us to part once and for all.

At this point, it seems appropriate to ask, since George is no longer with us, how did he himself actually fare when death came for him on November 29, 2001? Was he prepared for his own death at the relatively young age of fifty-eight years? Did he successfully practice the art of dying?

His family and closest friends have been mostly tight-lipped about his final days. George valued his privacy, and those around him have honored that. We know little more than he died in the house of a friend in Los Angeles, with his wife and son present. We are not, however, wholly in the dark. There are at least three facts to consider.

First, George knew that his cancer was probably going to kill him months before it finally took him, so he had plenty of time to reflect upon his fate. During that period he recorded his last song, "Horse to Water," which appears on Jools Holland's *Small World, Big Band*. It is credited to "RIP Ltd. 2001." On the assumption that George himself, as has been reported, was responsible for this tag, it is a good sign that his humor was intact until the end. It is clear enough from "Wreck Of The Hesperus" that George accepted growing older with grace. He likewise seems to have been able to laugh even as he saw death approaching.

Second, upon George's death, the Harrison family released this short but instructive statement: George "left this world as he lived in it: conscious of God, fearless of death and at peace, surrounded by family and friends. He often said: 'Everything else can wait but the search for

God can't wait, and love one another.'" His wife Olivia, in an interview sometime later, reiterated the point: "George dedicated a lot of his life to obtain a good ending, and I don't have any doubt that he was successful.... He gave his life to God a long time ago. He wasn't trying to hang on to anything. He was fine with it."

Third, we have a similar statement from a source outside the family. Shortly after George's death, his friend, Deepak Chopra, said in an interview: "I know that he died very conscious of God and in peace and not afraid of death"; George "had totally accepted his death, and was at peace with it, and unafraid of it." As Chopra was in a position to know the facts firsthand, it appears that George did indeed die with fortitude and calm, that he managed to attain what Catholic Christians have traditionally called a *bona mors*—a good or happy death.

In July of 2001, when rumors of his ill health were proliferating, George issued a brief statement asking his fans not to worry about him. By that point he almost certainly knew that he was dying. By asking others not to worry, I believe that he was trying to impart to them his own attitude. That is, he himself was not worried. It is not just that he had resigned himself to the fact that his life was almost over but that, in his own mind, he was headed for the light.

Notes

1. Taken from a 1982 interview of George by Mukunda Goswami, available online at: www.krishna.org/Articles/2000/08/00066.html.

2. The words to "Simply Shady" are very close to the prose on page 180 of George Harrison, *I, Me, Mine* (San Francisco: Chronicle Books, 2002): "We have to first of all not create more Karma—that is, more actions and reactions—like throwing a pebble into a clear lake, the ripples keep on going. Every thought, word, action or deed that we have is like sending a ripple out across the Universe and it does eventually come back. Whatever you do, it comes right back on you."

3. Paramahansa Yogananda, *Autobiography of a Yogi* (Los Angeles: Self-Realization Fellowship, 1990), 320.

4. The image is from George's tradition. See e.g. Yogananda, *Autobiography of a Yogi*, 489: "the ever-joyous Sea of Bliss," "the One Cosmic Ocean."

5. Yogananda, *Autobiography of a Yogi*, 309–22.

6. Harrison, *I, Me, Mine*, 180–81.

7. Harrison, *I, Me, Mine*, 180.

7

Brainwashed
HUMAN FOLLY

*I*n 1966 the Beatles recorded John Lennon's LSD-inspired "Rain." The song opens by observing that some people run and hide when it rains, and that they seek shade when the sun comes out. The singer represents himself as an individual who, to the contrary, doesn't mind the weather at all, rain or shine. (When George, in "Mystical One," claims that he's happy "shine or rain sitting here by a stream," he may echo "Rain.") Lennon then seemingly attempts to help his listeners. Repeating three times, "I can show you," he offers that things aren't really any different when it rains, just as they aren't really any different when the sun hits us with its rays. The point seems to be that perception is relative, that awareness of change is merely "a state of mind," and that various states of mind are possible. Lennon's voice leaves us with a thrice-asked query, "Can you hear me?"

THE LOVE THERE THAT'S SLEEPING

Further interpretation of this song doesn't matter for our purposes. All that requires our attention is the distinction "Rain" makes between insiders and outsiders, between those who know and those who don't know. The first half of the song discriminates between "they"—those who foolishly run and hide when the weather shifts—and the singing "I" who understands. This "I" grasps that, when rain comes or the sun appears, nothing really changes, and so he doesn't need shelter. The second half of the song similarly distinguishes between "I"—the wise man who can teach others if they'll only listen—and "you"—the potential learners, now ignorant.

"Rain," however musically delightful, is thoroughly condescending. The singer knows something important that regular people don't. He has been granted insight, and it's now his privilege to share what he's discovered with unenlightened others. It isn't clear, however, that they're capable of learning so much. When Lennon asks more than once, "Can you hear me?," he seems to be saying: I understand; you don't; maybe you never will. The conclusion is unavoidable: my state of mind is special, and your state of mind is inferior.

The patronizing attitude of Lennon's "Rain" as well as its bifurcation between the enlightened and the unenlightened have numerous parallels in George's music. One sees this already in 1967's "Within You Without You," although here it's not "I" but "we" versus "they" and "you." The latter are people who live in illusion and don't see "the truth," people who are ignorant of the power of love. Such off-course individuals gain "the world" only to lose everything. The singer, knowing better, seeks to foster self-reflection by asking, much like Lennon in "Rain," "Are you one of them?" He then finishes by offering a promise of sorts: peace will come to those who can "see beyond" themselves and recognize that "we're all one."

George's "Within You Without You" represents a sort of modern Gnosticism, by which I mean it presupposes a worldview in which the few as opposed to the many have received vital salvific insight into the true nature of things. Most people remain ignorant and so are lost.

This pessimistic take on things runs throughout George's lyrics. The singer of "Isn't It A Pity" is forlorn because so many can't appreciate the beauty around them, and he regrets that "not too many people" have grasped the truth that everyone's "the same." In "Devil's Radio," he feels resigned: "I don't know how you can't see." In "That's The Way It Goes," after speaking about the fire that destroys falsehood and which manifests itself in "the spiritual eye," he confesses that "you won't understand the way I feel." In "This Is Love"—which is not about human affection but the Divine-human encounter—love makes fools of all who just don't see the point. "That Which I Have Lost" remarks upon individuals who are wholly "bewildered" because they don't fathom the "law of action," by which George means the law of karma. The song also asserts that people—"you people"—need to have the "mirrors" of their "understanding" cleaned. (This is probably an allusion to Aldous Huxley's *The Doors of Perception*, his influential essay on drugs and enlightenment. Huxley was in turn alluding to a line from the poet William Blake.)

George's recurrent assertion that people—seemingly most people—don't understand is less a statement about the messenger than his message. The singer's point isn't personal. He isn't saying, "No one appreciates me." He is rather being metaphysical: people are alienated from God. There are, to be sure, exceptions. The heartfelt "My Guitar Can't Keep From Crying" objects that critics of the 1974 tour are victims of "ignorance" and "hate." This is not, however, the usual fare. When George remarks that people don't understand, or that they are hateful (as in "The Light That Has Lighted The World"), what he usually means is that they don't perceive the hidden nature of reality, or that they suspect the truth yet reject it.

If George often claims to know what the vast swath of humanity has yet to realize, he also, again like Lennon, can indulge in fierce criticism of others (although there is nothing as personal and spiteful as Lennon's dreadful and childish attack on Paul, "How Do You Sleep?," for which George, regrettably, played the guitar[1]). George, for example, unkindly sings from quite a lofty perch in "Piggies," on *The Beatles (The White Album)*. Although the lyrics are among his least thoughtful, they are still instructive. The musically mediocre contribution appears to mock members of what so many in the sixties dubbed "the establishment." "Piggies" are people of the privileged classes who have wealth and yet complain about their lot, who have power and yet fail to care for others. George doesn't try to understand them—not an ounce of empathy emerges from him. He neither wonders how they came to be what they are nor asks himself, as well he might, whether he'd be just like them if his circumstances had been different. Nor does he offer any friendly advice; he'd rather leave them where they are, sarcastically categorizing these self-centered human beings as "piggies," as though they belonged to another species entirely. Their kind is not his kind. "What they need's a damn good whacking."

Given the rest of George's musical corpus and what we otherwise know about him, it would be foolish to find in the sophomoric "Piggies" any real depth of malice. The song was a knockoff. One nonetheless understands why the insane Charles Manson, who unlike George was filled with hatred, could make the song his own. He reportedly often quoted the line about "whacking," and two of his murdered victims were, with a nod to George's last line ("clutching forks and knives"), stabbed with knife and fork. Moreover, Susan Atkins, one of Manson's devotees, used Sharon Tate's blood to write "Pigs" on the front door of Roman Polanski's house.

George's self-professed membership among the enlightened few as opposed to the unenlightened many and his ability to confess the sins of others, including their religious sins, are surely for many the least attractive features of his musical legacy. Critics can find and have found here a lack of generosity, even a spirit of arrogance. They have heard George singing down to them. He plays the disdainful and smug cynic, proclaiming the truth, though everyone else is a liar. Even those of us who find George generally edifying may in this matter have some second thoughts. He not only knows what's best for us, but he can in addition sound misanthropic, as in "Sunshine Life For Me (Sail Away Raymond)," where he claims that "most folks" just bore him, and that he would prefer a tree in a cornfield to their company.

Two albums in particular dispense George's harsh criticism of others. The first is *Somewhere In England*. It skewers record executives ("Blood From A Clone"). It ridicules those who go to discothèques ("Unconsciousness Rules"). It laments how many failed to understand what John Lennon was really saying ("All Those Years Ago"). It observes that "you people" can't find the time to seek illumination of consciousness or the renewal of their minds ("That Which I Have Lost"). It also warns that military threats are escalating while "big business" is destroying wildlife; in short, people with "evil hearts" are wrecking the earth ("Save The World"). The album in its entirety leaves us with the impression that George is alienated from those who have made the planet such a dire mess. It also plainly implies that the mess is everyone else's fault.

One finds more of the same on *Brainwashed*. "Any Road," to which we shall need to return later, preaches about those who don't know where they're going, so that it doesn't make any difference what path they're on. "P. 2 Vatican Blues," as we saw in chapter 4, mocks the Roman Catholic Church. "Rising Sun" speaks about "villains" and people who follow "the devil." And the closing "Brainwashed" is largely a lengthy list of the people and institutions that have "turned out the spiritual light" and made the world a "mess"—schools, teachers, kings, queens, stock exchanges, banks, governments, the media, the military, the press, and technocrats with their gadgets. On this album, the whole world has gone to hell.

The cover art only reinforces this impression. Counting the front and back covers of the CD booklet, twelve of the sixteen pages depict a family of dummies—pale, expressionless mannequins—who watch a flickering TV and absentmindedly gaze at news factoids about money. Clearly they live superficial lives; their hearts and minds are nowhere. They are, indeed, as George says over and over again in the final song, "brainwashed."

Before seeking to understand George's frequently critical spirit and his brand of what I have called "Gnosticism"—two things that go hand in hand—I should like, if only briefly, to take note of some particulars that draw George's ire. We saw, in an earlier chapter, how often he gives us political and social commentary, and that on these matters his opinions—war is evil, big business is bad, the environment is doomed—are largely derivative. They reflect little more than the counterculture of the 1960s. George does, however, submit some criticisms that are more than leftovers from the heydays of the sixties protesters.

First of all, he is critical of nightlife, of partying and drinking to excess. "Unconsciousness Rules" addresses itself to someone who can "dance the pants off of everyone" at "the discotheque." This individual is pale, his clothes are a mess, he looks half dead—in short, he's a "wreck." George's evaluation is that he's lost a screw in his head. He's an idiot.

This is not just George's take on seventies disco, although it certainly includes that. "Beware Of Darkness," on *All Things Must Pass*, already warns of falling "swingers," and "Devil's Radio," while observing that George himself doesn't "hang out much," affirms that the devil is in "the clubs and bars."

George's rejection of partying, we may observe, is bound up with the singer's unhappy firsthand knowledge of the dangers of alcohol and drugs. On "Try Some Buy Some," the singer mentions that he's seen people "die to get high." Whoever he has in mind there, he personally witnessed the toll drugs and drink took on John Lennon, Ringo Starr, and Eric Clapton. Perhaps this fact lies behind "Writing's On The Wall," where we hear of friends being "drunk away," that is, of drink disrupting intimate relationships. Further, George himself had—at least until the mid-1970s—his own troubles. "Simply Shady" recalls occasions when its singer went crazy after sipping from "the juicer" or fell down because of "the bottle," and "You And Me" (coauthored with Beatles' road manager Mal Evans and given to Ringo Starr for his 1973 self-titled *Ringo*) pleads guilty to "getting high" in nightclubs. It's interesting to learn that "Just For Today" is in fact a rewrite of an Alcoholics Anonymous brochure George had read.[2] It's also instructive that "Horse To Water," the last song George recorded, is a disquieting reflection on someone who "would like a drink." This person thirsts not for truth but for alcohol. George can see that he's in misery and that what he really needs is wisdom. But George hasn't been able to give him any. For the man has turned on his concerned friend. Downing another bottle, he has deluded himself that everything will be OK.

In addition to partying, a second thing George is down on is the media, which he regards as a vehicle of little more than gossip. The clearest demonstration of this is "Devil's Radio." This jumpy tune, which got less radio play than one might have expected, begins and ends by repeating the word "gossip" four times. In between we are told that "the devil's radio" is in clubs, bars, films, songs, magazines—"your magazines," not "our magazines"—and TV (which George also takes a swipe at in "Wrack My Brain," a song he gave to Ringo Starr to record). "The devil's radio" is predatory ("like vultures") and "thoughtless."

The song is much more than Don Henley's "Dirty Laundry," more than another easy assault on the journalistic media. It's not just George complaining that he can no longer spend a peaceful time at a decent restaurant ("make us hide behind shades"). We find the key to "Devil's Radio," I suggest, in a book written by one of George's heroes, *Autobiography of a Yogi* by Paramahansa Yogananda, in which the author asserts that "the Old Testament prophets called maya by the name of Satan.... The Greek Testament, as an equivalent for Satan, uses *diabolos* or devil." The devil is a magician who "produces multiplicity of forms to hide the One Formless Verity. In God's plan and play . . . the sole function of Satan or Maya is an attempt to divert man from Spirit to matter, from Reality to unreality."[3] "Devil's Radio" is, when read in the light of Yogananda's equation, not about the devil of the Christian tradition but instead about *mâya*, the Hindu principle of illusion. George is telling us that our popular culture, including its news media, is filled with profound illusion, with things that don't matter and don't last. The media—which The Beatles already implicitly criticized in "A Day In The Life"—may pretend to disperse important information, but they don't. Reality is somewhere else. The media crowd our lives with little but lies and empty gossip. George wants nothing to do with them.[4]

If the "Devil's Radio" is, on *Cloud Nine*, George's figure of speech for *mâya*, on his last album his chief metaphor for *mâya* is brainwashing. We have already observed that the art on the booklet depicts dummies who watch TV, which is the most important conduit of the modern media. Clearly these dummies are wasting their empty lives in an illusory world. The lyrics of several songs underline the theme of not understanding ("Any Road," "Pisces Fish," "Rising Sun") while the final song, "Brainwashed," disparages both "the media" and "the press." Those "who have the devil for a guide" ("Rising Sun") are victims of *mâya*, which the media spread abroad.

This leads us to a third complaint George often registers, and it is the circumstance he worries about most. What, to his mind, has been the upshot of our brainwashing and of our listening to "the devil's radio"? We are not just victims of ignorance and illusion in general but victims of religious ignorance and illusion in particular. Misled by *mâya*, we have become estranged from the Deity. In "The Day The World Gets 'Round," George observes that only "a few" bow before God or pray in silence. In "All Those Years Ago," he grumbles that "they've forgotten all about God." On "Brainwashed," he moans that the world is dark because its "spiritual light" has been extinguished. And so it goes. George sounds a bit like a fundamentalist Christian protesting the removal of God from this or that sphere of modern life. He believes that God matters above everything else, and he can't fathom those—in his eyes the majority—who seem to get by on what to him is the thin gruel of a purely secular existence.

Having canvassed some of the protests George makes, it might seem that we should be even less happy with him, for doesn't he himself stand guilty of some of the same sins he espies in others? He certainly did his fair share of partying and drinking, even into the mid-1970s. Again, while George's music criticizes record producers and the media, he made his life off of them. He owed his initial fame and fortune to the unprecedented publicity surrounding The Beatles, and he continued throughout his musical career to use the media for his own gain. He submitted to interviewers and appeared on radio and posed for pictures to promote his products.[5] How then can his lyrics be so critical of TV and the radio, which benefited him so much? Isn't this hypocrisy?[6]

Similarly, how can the author of "Taxman," who lived in a mansion and had a second home in Hawaii and who in general enjoyed the luxurious life of a millionaire, scold greedy businesspeople? Or how can George the movie producer assert that the devil is in films? It's certainly not because his own cinematic productions, which included the universally panned *Shanghai Surprise*, were invariably thoughtful or religiously beneficial.

One might also observe in this connection that George was very much taken with auto racing (and also loved expensive automobiles and driving them too fast). His love for and involvement with this sport are reflected in the self-titled *George Harrison*, which features "Faster." The jacket cover informs us that the song was "inspired by Jackie Stewart and Niki Lauda"—two famous race car drivers—and is "dedicated to the entire Formula One Circus." The artwork for the album shows George walking with the famous Stewart at a Grand Prix, and the promotional video George made for the song has Stewart driving the musician around in a limo. But, one might ask the pious George, isn't auto racing just another loud and dangerous material diversion, the sort of thing that keeps our minds preoccupied with matters other than God? Surely a religious type might fairly consider it to be rather empty, as lacking profundity or meaning. Are its devotees obviously superior to those whom George criticizes because they love to dance or go to the movies?

How George himself might have responded to these and like questions, and to what extent he may have humbly thought them partly fair—I like to imagine that he would have conceded that they have some force—we don't know.[7] I do, however, believe that we can at least make out some of the reasons why he had a proclivity for critical pronouncements and why he so often perceived the human race to be divided between the enlightened and the unenlightened.

I begin by observing that George is a well-known personality type. In his classic book, *The Varieties of Religious Experience*, William James discusses religious individuals whom he dubs the "twice-born,"[8] defining them partly by drawing a contrast with the "once-born." The latter are individuals who feel that all is right with the world. They tend to dispense cheer and to discount the darker aspects of life. They are optimistic about matters both great and small.

It's otherwise with the "twice-born." These sadder people, disenchanted with everyday life, feel the full weight of the world's evils, including their own sinful shortcomings. They are well aware that most people, whatever profession they make to the contrary, are only intermittently happy, or as Thoreau famously put it, that they "lead lives of quiet desperation." The twice-born further fail to find much comfort or satisfaction in material goods and the unstable affairs of this vain life. The ever-present realities of misfortune, illness, and death hold their attention. They are impressed by disappointment and anxiously sense the threat of emptiness everywhere. Pain seems to them an integral part of the world, not a temporary aberration that may soon disappear. The result is pessimism and melancholy, and such individuals may readily become alienated from the world. Solid reality can seem to them to be "remote, strange, sinister, uncanny," even unreal, as though one were perceiving it through a cloud—which perhaps corresponds with the experience George relates in "Stuck Inside A Cloud" and alludes to elsewhere, as in "Sunshine Life For Me," where a cloud hangs over him, and in "Blow Away," where a religious experience disperses the clouds gathered around him. The twice-born, before finding salvation, may even feel so estranged and desperate that life seems close to meaningless.

But the twice-born are no longer once-born. Persuaded that "the unreality cannot be" the true nature of things, that "a mystery" must be "concealed, that a metaphysical solution must exist," and that we must have some home other than this unhomelike world, the twice-born have longed for help—for help that the world, the source of the problem, cannot give. They have cried out for "a life not correlated with death, a health not liable to illness, a kind of good that will not perish, a good in fact that flies beyond the goods of nature." And they believe they have been favored, through a supernatural deliverance, with just this. A reality beyond themselves has delivered them from an unfulfilled existence and given them a new start and instilled a deeper level of consciousness. Having died to the old life, they have been begotten into a new life. And having become assured of their own salvation, they now see the potential salvation of the entire world. Worry declines. They can now enjoy peace and perceive harmony. Feeling connected with a larger, universal power, they are no longer ruled by melancholy, and it is possible for them to revel in the beauty of nature and to move beyond themselves to care for the whole world. Often, and naturally enough, the twice-born can become evangelistic about all this, ardently wanting others to know what they now know.

It should be obvious to anyone familiar with George's life or music that, by and large, he seems to be a good example of James's twice-born. His music records the agony, doubt, and estrangement so typical of such people. It equally, as we have seen throughout this book, records the joy of finding God, preaches the need for the renewing of ones' consciousness, conveys the splendor of the natural world, and dispenses the imperative to care for others. George's music, then, features two selves—the old self without or before God and the new self with or after God. This is almost certainly the theme of "Try Some Buy Some" (which, incidentally, David Bowie covered for his 2003 *Reality*).[9] Here George tells us that once he had nothing, that once he saw nothing, that once he was lonely, that once he felt nothing, and that once he knew nothing. Now, however, his eyes are opened, because "I called on your love, and your love came to me." Although George's comments on this in *I, Me, Mine* are in my opinion close to incoherent,[10] he does at least acknowledge that, for him, the song is "spiritual." This is sufficient prod for us to infer that here we are listening to George the saved looking back on George the unsaved.

The circumstance of having been twice-born helps us greatly in understanding George's critical spirit as well as his basic demarcation between those who understand and those who don't understand. Individuals who have an earlier and later self, with the dividing line being profound religious experience, inevitably project their own autobiographical rift onto the world. They know from personal experience that there are two sorts of lives, the empty and the full, the natural and the supernatural, and they see the world accordingly: If I have been two people, there must be two sorts of people—those who have, like me, been born twice and become enlightened, and those who have not. In this way the story of one's life becomes the story of the world. Others are either like my current, enlightened self, or they are like my earlier, unenlightened self.

George once said: "I'd rather be one of the devotees of God than one of the straight, so-called sane or normal people who just don't understand that man is a spiritual being, that he has a soul."[11] Here George unambiguously divides the world into two sorts—the devotees of God, and those who don't understand spiritual realities. The dualism, the perception that some know and that some don't know, is, I am suggesting, the natural outcome of George's biography.

George's own story is also the source of his feeling that the world is a stage featuring a great battle between good and evil, between darkness and light. If one was formerly in unhappy darkness but now sees the divine light, it seems to follow that there are two antagonistic forces loose in the world. George said as much in an interview: "In this physical world we live in there's always duality—good and bad, black and white, yes and no. Whatever there is, there's always the opposite. There's always something equal and something opposite to everything. . . ."[12] This proposition has its musical counterpart in "Any Road," where the singer muses about the thoughts in his head moving between "the dark and the light."

George's dualism is, as just indicated, an ethical dualism, for light is good, darkness bad. And this is the presupposition of much of his criticism of others. It's not just that he dislikes in others what he, in retrospect, sees as having once been his own sins, but further that he perceives the world as a dark and dangerous place, and he must do battle with those who, even if unconsciously, obscure the divine light.

One may at this point protest that George doesn't objectively perceive the world as it is, for our world is filled with shades of gray. But the twice-born are in one crucial respect just like the rest of us: we all interpret the world in terms of our own experience. Nothing else is possible. And when one has encountered a profoundly new level of consciousness that seems a vast advance over the normal, everyday state of consciousness, how can this not change one's view of everything? If, moreover, one soon enough discovers that one's most important experiences and deepest beliefs are not shared by everyone, how will one not think something like what the Gospels say: "Many are called but few are chosen"? Further, can we expect such twice-born people to be silent about the treasure they have discovered, or not to be critical of whatever prevents its discovery? Again, if one has found life with God so meaningful as to render meaningless one's earlier life without God, how will one avoid surmising that much human experience is misdirected and superficial, a whirl of delusion? And won't one further be persuaded that the true nature of things is unlike a city set on a hill, that the biggest truth of all can indeed be hid? Won't it be apparent that people miss the firm and lasting reality beneath the material world just as though they were mistaking the snow for the ground? All this seems endemic to the twice-born, and all this we find in George.

We should additionally keep in mind, when trying to understand George, that he studied Hinduism seriously, and the Hindu scriptures are full of remarks about there being two sorts of people, those who see and those who are blind. Those scriptures also plainly assert that, when people come into the world, they are insensible to the truth. Here is a brief sampling from one source, the *Bhagavad-Gita*:

- 7:3: "Among thousands of people, perhaps one strives for perfection, and of those who strive and succeed scarcely one knows Me [Krishna] in truth."
- 7:13: "Deluded . . . this whole world doesn't recognize Me who am above them and imperishable" (Krishna).

- 7:25: "Veiled by My creative power, I [Krishna] am not revealed to all. This bewildered world knows Me not, the unborn, the unchanging."
- 7:26: "Me [Krishna] no one knows."
- 7:27: "All beings are born deluded, O Bharata (Arjuna), overcome by the dualities which arise from wish and hate."
- 16:16: "Led astray by many wrong thoughts, entangled in the net of delusion, enchained to the pleasures of their cravings, they fall down into a foul hell."

That George took lines such as these to heart is beyond all doubt. The first verse I have quoted, from *Bhagavad-Gita* 7:3, is the quotation George selected for the frontispiece of his autobiography, *I, Me, Mine*. So his dualism and critical pessimism belong to his religious tradition. We shouldn't expect him to show us anything else.

Before bringing this chapter to a close, I should like to consider two additional factors that encourage us to be sympathetic with George despite his often superior posturing and censorious spirit. The first is that he was undoubtedly to some extent a victim of his own celebrity, and the hype and madness that enveloped The Beatles must have distorted his perception of the world and of its ordinary citizens. George the introvert was overwhelmed by Beatlemania, by all the unprecedented attention and his subsequent inability to lead any sort of normal life. Crazed fans trailed and mobbed him and his three bandmates wherever they went. Concert audiences screamed so loud that the music went unheard, a circumstance George despised. (A memorable record of this absurdity is preserved in the concert footage of The Beatles at Shea Stadium on August 15, 1965. At one point Lennon gives up playing the notes and just slides his elbow up and down his electric piano, and it makes no difference at all.)

All the mindless adulation bordered on frenzied worship, and as the object of such idolization, George well knew how hollow and silly it was. Craving normalcy, he went to India, hoping to get away from the insanity, only to find that even there he was a celebrity, a magnet for excitable crowds.

Such crowds could be scary. Early one night at The Cavern in Liverpool a man accosted George and head-butted him in the face.

Later the madness was such that all of The Beatles sometimes worried whether their very lives were in danger. As we all know, it turned out that a mad assassin took John Lennon's life; and in 1999 a similarly disturbed intruder managed to beat the security at George's mansion in Henley on Thames, Oxfordshire, and came close to killing him. How could all this not make George a bit jaded or skeptical of large portions of the human race? He knew that the adulatory mobs were, to borrow his phrase from "Someplace Else," really "empty faces," and that a few of them were even dangerous. My guess is that when the song "Brainwashed" reports that "they even got my grandma, while she was working for the mob," the word "mob" refers not to organized crime but to the madness of crowds.

While reflection on George's rowdy and sometimes unsettling public may reduce how much offense we take at his judgmental temperament, another consideration moves us to be even more kindly disposed to him: George's criticism of others is neatly balanced by criticism of himself. Sometimes, moreover, when he is censuring others, he is really worrying about himself. Songs ostensibly addressed to others are often aimed at himself and are in truth a form of self exhortation.

The touching "Hear Me Lord," on *All Things Must Pass*, is relevant in this connection. Here George prays that his Lord will forgive people who "feel they can't afford you." But this prayer for others without God comes only after a very different prayer: "Forgive me Lord." The singer is asking forgiveness for all the years he himself ignored God. The poetic parallelism entails that George is not, after all, so different from those who don't see things his way. He's acutely conscious that he was once like them, and that he, too, requires forgiveness. Everyone is in the same human boat.

The awareness that he once lived without God and, more importantly, that he has, since finding God, failed to live up to his own religious aspirations, are regular themes in George's music. As we have already seen in chapter 2, he is not bashful about confessing his own sins, pre- or post-conversion. The list of dirty laundry in "Headed For The Light" is not atypical.

That George is the object of his own complaints and exhortations is evident above all on *Brainwashed*. This album, as we have seen, is one of his most cynical and most critical. At the same time, if one gives it a careful listening, it's also very self-critical. George is as full of failings as the rest of us. His advice is accordingly not for others only.

In the opening song, "Any Road," the pronouns are all mixed up. George sings to "you," as in the refrain: "if you don't know where you're going, any road will take you there." But this "you" alternates with the singer's "I." George, too, has been traveling, and doing so in many different vehicles. Furthermore, this "I" doesn't pretend that, while others may be ignorant, he's known exactly where he's going. On the contrary, three times he joins himself to his audience by using "we." Twice he says that "we pay the price," and once he says that "we've got to fight." In this way, George joins the rest of us. He too has had to pay for his failings, and he too must fight the good fight because he has not yet ended his journey.

The pronouns also get jumbled in "Pisces Fish." Here George—again using "I"—sings about his "soul," through which the divine river runs, and he anticipates ultimately enjoying the infinite sea of divine bliss. At the same time, he lets us know that this river also runs through "your parents," and he adds that it's easy "for us to miss." The significance of the "us" instead of "you" appears from two subsequent lines. In one, George wonders whether "we"—not "you" or "they"—have time to sort out the mysteries of what life is all about. In the other line, in the closing stanza, he declares that he himself is "living proof" of all of the "contradictions" with which life confronts us. He follows with the remark that half of him is going where his other half has already gone. These words presumably reflect George's self-conception as a Pisces, the astrological sign for which is that of two fish facing opposite directions. George's application of this image to himself is that he is a divided man. Perhaps he's even suggesting he has a religious and nonreligious self.

However that may be, George's personal piety doesn't measure up to his own standard in the next song, "Looking For My Life," his moving memoir of the 1999 attack on his life. This is a self-revealing prayer in which George mourns his distance from his Lord. We overhear him say that he's got to "get back" to God, and that he's somehow become "stuck." He also admits that death's nearness made clear to him his lack of preparation, indeed revealed that he didn't know where he was "headed." This is not just a statement that the attack surprised him but a candid admission that, at the time, his life with God wasn't what it should've been. In other words, George was among the disoriented, those not knowing where they're going, those described earlier on "Any Road." When he adds that he never obtained any "GCEs"—"GCE" being the abbreviation for "General Certificate of Education"—this is not a statement about his academic career but a figurative way of confessing an ignorance that led to religious waywardness. In line with this, the CD booklet, in printing the lyrics, capitalizes the last word of the refrain in its last occurrence, making it into a proper noun—"Looking for my Life." The capitalized "Life" must stand for the Divinity, so in this song George has, in one sense, not found God but is still seeking God.

"Rising Sun" comes next. Its first two stanzas introduce us to the world as seen through Hindu eyes. "The devil"—which, I have argued, stands for *mâya*—leads people around, with the result that they are nervous, full of guilt, and confined to the material world ("crippled by boundaries"). The world is like a room filled with mirrors, in which everything is distorted and disguised—again a reference to the power of *mâya*. Then George sings that the "rising sun"—God—is "inside of you." Here the divinity is in George's listeners, even if they don't know it. Later in the song George changes this to "inside of me." Before we get to that, however, we have a whole stanza exposing George's own flaws. He owns up that he'd been working on the road of "sinners," and further that it had almost destroyed him. He was saved only because "a signal" graciously came to him and brought him back to life. While George doesn't inform us what precisely this signal was, his general meaning is obvious. He is telling us that, at some recent point in time, he had in important respects misplaced his religious life. Only lately has he found it again, so that he once more feels the divine life always rising within him.

Following "Rising Sun" is "Stuck Inside A Cloud." One might initially take this to be an ordinary love song, a description of George's desolation at being separated from his lover: he lacks sleep and is smoking too much and is crying because she has left him. But this is not what "Stuck Inside A Cloud" is about. The giveaway is the singer's expressed desire that he might touch the "lotus feet" of the one he's addressing. This refers to the blessed feet of a religious teacher, saint, or divinity. George is trying to reconnect to God, either directly or through a religious intermediary. Although the song is sufficiently obscure that one can't say much more than this, it is at least clear that George is mourning his current relationship with God. One shouldn't miss the use of "stuck" in the title. This takes us back to "Looking For My Life," which has to do with the same or a similar religious predicament ("I feel so stuck that I can't get to you").

The concluding song on the album is "Brainwashed." In this George has an explicit theological lesson to impart. In the middle of the song he quotes from *How to Know God*: "The soul does not love. It is love itself. It does not exist. It is existence itself. It does not know. It is knowledge itself."[13] These words express the Hindu conviction about ultimate reality, and they entail *mâya* because the assertions go against all appearances: things are not what they appear to be. But the interesting fact is that, although the song is accusatory, once more the pronouns vary. Although twice we hear the words, "brainwash you," once "you're brainwashed," this alternates with being brainwashed in "our childhood" and by "our teachers," "our leaders," and "our Kings and Queens." "Brainwashed us" also occurs a full four times; and when George identifies God as the wisdom "we seek" or the lover whom "we miss," he positions himself as one who has not yet found, or who has lost what he had found earlier. It is also noteworthy that he asks God to lead "us"—not "them"—through the world's mess. He even admits that what everyone is searching for is "something I forgot." Here George leaves the company of the enlightened. He's just like the rest of us.

Although the album *Brainwashed* is accusatory in general, it equally accuses George. As we have already seen the same phenomenon on "Hear Me Lord," which was on George's first solo album, awareness of his own deficiencies spans his entire recording career. So I believe that some of George's critics have been unfair to him. He can indeed get preachy, but the sermons are aimed at himself as well as the rest of us. He may know himself to be twice-born, but he also recognizes, from painful experience, that this is not the remedy to everything. Life goes on, and the new self never completely exorcizes the old self. The two selves rather go through life in the material world together, ever in tension, sometimes at war. At times one self dominates, at other times the other has the upper hand. Perhaps that is why George calls himself a contradiction. He is not one but two.

Because George witnesses within himself a struggle between light and darkness, his chief response to the world must, in the end, be pity, not condemnation—otherwise he would have to condemn himself. He may have laid hold of the answer to life's mysteries, but his hands are slippery. So he must again and again reach out for "That Which I Have Lost." George is not the soul triumphant but the soul careworn and inconstant. That is why his guitar gently weeps. "The love that lies sleeping" sometimes slumbers within George himself.

Notes

1. Some animosity toward the other Beatles does, however, come to expression in "Not Guilty" and "Sue Me, Sue You Blues"; and in the late 1960s George was often angry with Paul. He blamed him for keeping Harrisongs off Beatles albums.

2. See George's comments in his *Creem* interview, December 1987 and January 1988.

3. Paramahansa Yogananda, *Autobiography of a Yogi* (Los Angeles: Self-Realization Fellowship, 1990), 322.

4. George's extreme dislike of the media appears from his 1982 hyperbolic comment that "the media is to blame for everything." See the interview by Mukunda Goswami, available online at: www.krishna.org/Articles/2000/08/00066.html.

5. In his *Creem* interview (December 1987/January 1988), he is quite clear that he hopes *Cloud Nine* will sell well and get a lot of airplay.

6. Although he allowed Chrysler to utilize "Something" for an auto commercial, he did to his credit turn down commercial requests to use "Here Comes The Sun."

7. According to Joshua M. Greene, *Here Comes the Sun: The Spiritual and Musical Journey of George Harrison* (Hoboken, NJ: John Wiley & Sons, 2006), 246, George thought that the best race car drivers had an expanded form of consciousness. If so, this might have helped him somehow link auto racing with spirituality.

8. William James, *The Varieties of Religious Experience* (New York: New American Library, 1958), 112–206.

9. In a *Rolling Stone* interview designed to promote his album, Bowie stated that all four Beatles contributed to George's song. I am unaware of any supporting evidence for his statement.

10. In passing, it's amusing to learn that George's "Try Some Buy Some" was a remake of a 1971 single he wrote and produced for Ronnie Spector, and that Spector, in her autobiography, *Be My Baby: How I Survived Mascara, Miniskirts, and Madness, Or My Life as a Fabulous Ronette* (New York: Harper-Perennial, 1990), 184, recalls that, when George asked her what she thought of the song, she didn't know what to say because she didn't know what it was about—"Religion? Drugs? Sex? I was mystified. And the more George sang, the more confused I got"—and she thought the song was "terrible." Her own dreadful rendition of the song didn't help matters.

11. Taken from a 1982 interview by Mukunda Goswami, available online at: www.krishna.org/Articles/2000/08/00066.html

12. Derek Taylor, *It Was Twenty Years Ago Today* (New York: Simon & Schuster, Inc., 1987), 127.

13. He gives the page number (130) but not publication details.

The Love There That's Sleeping

SALVATION

*E*very religion seeks to answer three fundamental questions. The first question, which implies discontent with the way things are, is: What is wrong with human beings? The second question, which summons hope, is: What is our ultimate destiny beyond this world? And the third question, which assumes a way from here to there, is: What enables us to be transformed so that we can get to where we ought to be?

George's lyrics supply answers to all three questions. They accordingly outline a religious scheme of salvation. His songs map for us the saving path from our current plight to the ideal state beyond the struggles of earthly existence. In brief:

1. Our problem is that our individual egos attach themselves to the material world. We should be tourists merely passing through. Tragically, we instead want to stay and set up housekeeping.

Engrossed with things that don't really matter, we become preoccupied with the visible, with the transient instead of the transcendent, and so we live "a life that isn't real" ("Be Here Now"). We mistake the material world, which is only a grand illusion, for the real world, and so we are lost.

2. Human destiny lies outside this fleeting, mundane reality. We know this because, among other reasons, we intuitively long for unification with God, the supreme reality. All else is, at best, prelude.

3. The illumination of consciousness is the means of our salvation. We can work for this end, with the help of God's grace, by engaging in devotional practices that foster a critical distance from the material world and so push us toward another and higher reality in which our union with God can be fully realized.

We have already, in previous chapters, touched upon all three points. Here I should like to consider what might awaken one to the human predicament in the first place. How do we come to realize that something is dreadfully amiss with the world as it is, and that we are indeed caged prisoners? And how is it that hope for something better may arise?

We know that, in George's own mind, the turning point for him came with drugs: he met God through LSD. Yet most of the others who took hallucinogens in the 1960s had very different experiences. LSD scarcely carried everyone to religious faith. It is natural, then, to infer that George was, even before experimenting with hallucinogens, somehow predisposed to embracing a spiritual view of life. To say much beyond that is hazardous. That there was, for example, any sort of personal crisis behind his coming to faith doesn't appear from the biographies; and it is, moreover, all but impossible to guess what unconscious role if any his childhood Catholicism played in his conversion.

Yet if we put to one side what we know about George's life and instead scrutinize his lyrics, we can discover at least one significant prod that, in his judgment, should encourage the rest of us to recognize the predicament that we are in, a predicament only some transcendent reality can resolve. That prod is simply this: day-to-day living in the material world is for the most part unfulfilling, so unless we are resigned to despair, it is natural to search for something more. As the happiness we seem programmed to find cannot be laid hold of in this lower world, we must discover it, if anywhere, elsewhere.

As George knows all too well, life on this planet often leaves us dissatisfied, even when we achieve the fame and fortune everyone seems to yearn for. In "Headed For The Light," the outwardly successful singer confesses that, instead of being comforted by his achievements, he's gone about "with nothing more than time" on his "hands." This is a clear acknowledgment of ennui, of moments when he's found himself with so little to do that he's become bored. "Miss O'Dell," the enigmatic and little-known flipside of "Give Me Love (Give Me Peace On Earth)," records the same feeling. In this biting exposé of his own celebrity status, George informs the listener—ostensibly Miss O'Dell, a friend who worked at Apple—that nothing at all new has happened since he last saw her and that he is bored to tears.

Then there is "(Can Only) Run So Far," which George probably wrote for Eric Clapton (who was the first to record it). The song is a very jaded look at fame. It speaks of "lonely days," "lonesome tears," and a "blue guitar." The moral of the piece seems to be that outward success can't cast out internal misery, and that people must live with themselves: no matter how far we run, we always bring ourselves along. We can't forsake ourselves.

Worldly accomplishment also fails to gratify in the jaunty "Wreck Of The Hesperus." Here George relates that he has met "some Oscars and Tonys," by which he means people who have won Oscars and Tonys. Such individuals clearly mean nothing to him. Those who step onto the merry-go-round of fortune and fame don't impress him at all because he knows from firsthand experience that all the promises are false: worldly achievement doesn't satisfy the longing of his soul. When George goes on to tell us that he has "met a snake climbing ladders," he is surely characterizing someone going up the so-called ladder of success. George's attitude is, Who cares? Although he was once at the top of the ladder himself, he tells us in "Cockamamie Business" that he never wished to be a celebrity; he just wanted to play his guitar. Outward success ultimately means nothing to George because it is not inward success.

The same indifference to, or implicit renunciation of, worldly success, the realization that it is a will-o'-the-wisp, appears in "That's The

Way It Goes," one of the more enjoyable songs on the commercially unsuccessful *Gone Troppo* (an album that one reviewer, with some justice, called "pathologically laid back"). This pleasing number, with its Indian-influenced slide sound, depicts three different individuals. Each is consumed by a desire for wealth and/or fame. The first has recently suffered a setback in the stock market and so is afraid. George seems to pity him. The second man dreams of using his wealth to buy property which he will then subdivide and resell at profit and in this way "feel his clout." George despises him. The third man is an actor looking for a starring role. But George thinks that the aspiring performer is blind, and he discerns in him nothing but "pose," that is, pretense. When George goes on to sing the titular refrain, "And that's the way it goes," he is communicating a sort of apathy. Neither profit nor loss counts for anything, and the same goes for fame. These are ephemeral, nothing but "lies." They certainly don't win us personal immortality. If there is anything that matters, it can't be what the three men in "That's The Way It Goes" are looking for. Speaking for himself, George declares that the important thing is having a "spiritual eye," about which the characters in his song know nothing. He is counseling us that we need above all the ability to perceive the transcendent reality that lies beyond the temporal and the mundane.

Success in obtaining money or worldly position, which is what we all have been brainwashed to chase, can leave one isolated. "Lay His Head," the B-side of "Got My Mind Set On You," knowingly affirms that the rich and famous never really know who their friends are. This is why George goes on to confide that he doesn't have a friend's shoulder to cry on. In "Wake Up My Love," he even complains that he has "no friends" at all, and this is why he's calling out to God. No doubt George is exaggerating here, but he certainly understands that the things people believe will make us happy are, as often as not, the things that will make us unhappy.

George's feeling of isolation from others also comes to clear expression in "Stuck Inside A Cloud," where he sings of talking to himself and says that he is the only one listening: "Only I can hear me." Ultimately, George is saying, we are all alone, notwithstanding all the success and adulation in the world. This is one reason why "Who Can See It" sums everything up by speaking simply of "this sad world." The unelaborated description interprets human existence as a whole as tragic. We live in what George, in the title of another song, calls a "World Of Stone." This is the dark, uncomfortable place where sadness and mourning always grow ("I Live For You"). Human existence, in the words of "Someplace Else," is full of "loneliness" and "empty faces." George at one point—perhaps recalling "The Ballad Of John And Yoko"—even thinks of himself as being metaphorically crucified ("See Yourself"). How can he not long to be "Someplace Else"? How can he ever imagine this world to be his true home? Ordinary life is empty. And it's all the worse if, as George believes, reincarnation is true, for then we must have lived "through a million years of crying" ("The Art Of Dying").

Just being alive is not enough. And just being busy is not enough. And even being successful or prosperous is not enough. We are all assailed by the problem and despair of "just being there" ("So Sad"). George, however, doesn't remain mired in his despair, because he just can't believe that that's all there is. He's aware of a persistent voice or restless feeling within which insists that human beings weren't created for tedium and misery and loneliness. Those depressing states somehow feel wrong. They aren't really supposed to be. They are foreign to our deepest nature. The result is an alienation from the self. We end up "bewildered" ("That Which I Have Lost"), and this ought to move us to aspire to something beyond the concrete world of the five senses. Goaded by a lack of personal fulfillment, we should long for something that the world can't give, something transcendent and nonmaterial.

For George, a "bottomless heart" has been implanted in human beings, and it remains restless until it finds its rest in something beyond or higher than the material world ("Poor Little Girl"). Indeed, George feels that somewhere inside himself is the desire to be "a perfect entity" ("The Art Of Dying").[1] At the foundation of his religiosity is an inbuilt feeling, which has become a doctrinal conviction, that the vast emptiness in human beings is there to be filled up by a vast something; and if nothing we run across in the material world is large enough to fill the hole, then there must be something beyond this lower world. It's this deeper yearning for more, this seemingly inborn tendency of his nature, that fuels George's religious journey and will not let him put his feet up here.

It's instructive at this point to recall George's personal history. He had been a Beatle, and as such he knew as much fame as anyone in the world. His musical career also brought him a great deal of money. (The rumors that he was suffering financial difficulties before the release of The Beatles' *Anthology* appear unsubstantiated.) So he had celebrity status galore and, most of his life, fortune enough. So when these two staples of popular aspiration didn't bring personal fulfillment, when they indeed left him empty and bored, it was obvious that no amount of notoriety or wealth would ever suffice.

Perhaps The Beatles implicitly conceded this when, at the height of their popularity, they decided to study Transcendental Meditation under the Maharishi Mahesh Yogi and then go off to India for some time in 1968. Their unprecedented, worldwide popular success taught them that, when you have what you want, you still don't have what you need. George explicitly acknowledged the failure of The Beatles' achievements to fulfill his deepest aspirations. In a 1982 interview he observed that after The Beatles had "been successful" and met "everybody" they "thought worth meeting," they discovered that such people really "weren't worth meeting." George and his bandmates "had more hit records than everybody else" and they did "it bigger than everybody else," and yet George didn't therewith find the promised land. His experience rather was "like reaching the top of a wall and then looking over and seeing that there's so much more on the other side. So I felt it was part of my duty to say, 'Oh, okay, maybe you are thinking this is all you need—to be rich and famous—but actually it isn't.'"[2]

George's personal experience of not being satisfied with his celebrity and affluence was part of what commended Hinduism to him and made it seem so intuitively plausible, for its teachings emphasize the uselessness of acquiring material things and the vanity of grabbing for the fleeting things of this world. The *Bhagavad-Gita* advises that we should be "without attachment" (3:7), that "craving" things is our enemy (3:37), that the "insatiable fire of desire" for this or that is the constant foe of "the wise" and "deludes the embodied soul" (3:39–40).

When George, recalling one of his Beatles compositions, entitled his autobiography, *I, Me, Mine*, he was being ironic. His first religious goal in life was to diminish his own ego and its craving nature. He wanted less I, less me, less mine, and he called the onerous struggle to achieve this "the eternal problem."³ The disparagement of "attachment" in "Woman Don't You Cry For Me," George's remark that it "only hurts you," is for him of the widest significance. Desiring more just leads to more desire, so it's truly "madness" ("Simply Shady"). I, me, and mine are a bottomless pit; only the Infinite can encompass and fill them.

So much for the human predicament and how one might become aware of it. What then should be one's goal, according to George? In "That Which I Have Lost," he asks for his "consciousness" to be illumined. This prayer is perhaps not surprising for one who grew up in the 1960s. There was then a lot of talk about "consciousness," about such things as "consciousness raising" and "altered states of consciousness." For George, however, such talk wasn't a passing fad. He forever remained eagerly desirous of expanding his "consciousness" and indeed believed that an illumined mind was his path to God.

But what exactly is an illumined mind or, to use the synonym on "Horse To Water," "God realization"? Ultimately it's becoming aware of our true natures, which means recognizing the presence of the Divinity who already lives within us. We're even now united with God. It's just that we don't perceive this stupendous fact, that the self contains something so vast and yet so concealed, and so we don't live out the reality. Material appearances deceive us and we don't become what we already are.

In "That's The Way It Goes," George sings that human beings "conceal all there is to know." While we vainly hunt to and fro for satisfaction, everything we need is already to hand, if only we could make out the truth. The solution to the human dilemma lies within because God lies within. It accords with this that George declares, in "Brainwashed," that the worst thing of all is "ignorance." The ignorance he has in mind is the widespread failure to sense and to respond to the supernatural life that flows on within us and without us ("Within You Without You"). Foolishly living according to the dictates of what George calls "the little 'I,'" we miss "the big 'I,'" the Supreme Consciousness behind all of reality, of which we are already a part.⁴

Perhaps the clearest statement in George's music of the kinship of the individual self (in Hinduism: Atman) to the Universal Self (Brahman) comes in "Brainwashed." One minute and fifty seconds into the song, the raucous hard rock gives way to a simple and serene slide guitar which falls into the background while a voice—identified in the CD booklet as Isabela Borzymowska—explicitly quotes from the book, *How to Know God*: "The soul does not love, it is love itself. It does not exist, it is existence itself. It does not know, it is knowledge itself." The individual soul, so far from being an orphan in the universe, shares divine attributes: love, Being, knowledge.

The same conviction may also be present, if to be sure much more subtly, in the earlier "If You Believe." Here George enjoins listeners to "get up" and then explains himself with the proposition, "you have all your needs." If the individual self somehow contains the Universal Self or is contained by it, then everything that we require has already been supplied. The kingdom of God is within. Self-actualization is God-realization.

In line with this, "If You Believe" speaks about belief in "you" as well as belief in "me" and indeed sets the two relevant statements in parallel to each other. If we identify the "me" with God instead of George, as seems natural, then it appears that the listeners' belief in themselves ("you") is correlated with their belief in God ("me"). Is this another way of saying that one finds God by finding the truth about one's own internal nature?

"Mystical One" is also intriguing in this connection. Here George says of himself, "I am." Not "I am this" or "I am that" but simply, "I am." The repetition—he uses the phrase four times—arrests our attention, and it's natural to surmise that maybe George is here playing on the biblical "I am," the name of God which Moses hears from the burning bush and which the Gospel of John has Jesus apply to himself. If George is in fact aware of the loaded use of the phrase in the Bible, he would seem, in daringly co-opting it for himself, to be affirming his affinity with God.

However that may be, George's mystical union with God is undeniable in "Sat Singing." We looked at this little-known but intriguing account of a profound religious ecstasy at some length in chapter 2. Here I call attention to the line in which George confides to us that he felt himself somehow becoming a "part" of God. His meaning is amplified later in the song, when he affirms that now "nothing separates" his life from his "goal," that goal of course being God. So George's

THE LOVE THERE THAT'S SLEEPING

Hindu doctrine—summarized in two famous phrases: "Ayam Atma Brahman" (= "I am Brahman") and "Tat Tvam Asi" (= "You are That")—is realized in his experience. He finds the Deity within himself and so comes to "God realization."

Acquaintance with mystical literature teaches that sometimes experiences like the one described in "Sat Singing" come out of the blue. It is also the case, however, that such experiences can be, through certain religious practices, partly stimulated or prepared for. George certainly thought so and was ever seeking to cultivate encounters with God. So what exactly did he think that one should be doing in order to foster "God realization"? In other words, once one has right knowledge—that is, once one has accepted basic Hindu beliefs ("If You Believe")—what is right practice? How does one overcome being ruled at all times by the unconscious and instead become open to perceiving that one is a container of God? George's lyrics extol at least three religious exercises:

1. The first is the incantation of God's names. George believed deeply in the efficacy of chanting, and the practice features prominently throughout his career. In 1968, he composed the instrumental "Singing Om" for the film *Wonderwall*. In 1969, George produced "The Hare Krishna Mantra" for the Radha Krishna Temple, which became a hit in the U.K. but not the U.S. "Awaiting on you all," on 1970's *All Things Must Pass*, promises that chanting the names of God will bring freedom, by which George means salvation from the material world. On the same album, "My Sweet Lord" incorporates most of the traditional Hare Krishna chant or Maha-mantra, the great chant for deliverance ("Hare Krishna, Hare Krishna, Krishna Krishna, Hare Hare, Hare Rama, Hare Rama, Rama Rama, Hare Hare"). "Give Me Love (Give Me Peace On Earth)," on *Living In The Material World*, which was released in 1973, has George chanting the sacred syllable, "OM," and this syllable also turns up two years later in *Extra Texture*'s "World Of Stone." In 1974, on *Dark Horse*, George repeatedly praises his God with "Jai (= Hail!) Krishna." For the cover of *Thirty Three & 1/3*, in 1976, the "3" is stylized to look like the Hindu symbol for "OM" (ॐ). In 1997, George produced and publicly promoted

Ravi Shankar's *Chants Of India*. Finally, the CD booklet for *Brainwashed*, George's farewell CD, has a cartoon figure meditating upon the words, "God, God, God," which is the refrain of the final song, "Brainwashed"; and that song ends with George chanting a long list of divine names.

The ex-Beatle nowhere in his lyrics explains chanting. He fails to clarify for instance how it should be done or how often. Nor does he inform us that it requires a pure heart or that it's designed to enable one to transcend the intellect; and he neglects either to elucidate that chanting is, in his Hindu tradition, much like a child calling for its mother or to elucidate precisely how it brings freedom to its practitioners. From interviews, however, we can fill in some of the blanks.[5] It's clear that George found chanting to be not only pleasant but, much more importantly, an effective way of entering into a deeper spiritual awareness, and that his thoughts on the subject are pretty much the standard teachings of the Hare Krishna movement.

Many of the sounds that daily assail our ears summon from us the desire to find temporary gratification in this or that material thing. But there are also special sounds, called mantras, which, at least according to the Vedic literature and Hindu tradition, are magical. They can work extraordinary ends, from physical healing and good luck to the expulsion of demons and the death of enemies. (On one occasion, while aboard an airplane that was in trouble, George desperately chanted and later told others that he may have thereby averted a crash.) The most important sounds of all, however, are those of the divine name, because they are conduits by which the Infinite Divinity chooses to enter the material world. Hindus have even said that the names of the Deity and the Deity are identical. So when one is mindfully and piously chanting, not just repeating words, one is literally in contact with God. Such contact with spiritual vibration, with transcendental sound, which is ultimately heard not by the outer ear but by the inner ear of enlightened beings, can foster ecstasy and produce long-lasting effects. As it says in Rupa Gosvami's fifteenth-century collection of poetry, *Padyavali*: "The holy name of Lord Krishna is an attractive feature for many. . . . It is the annihilator of all sinful reactions and is so powerful. . . . Save for the dumb who cannot chant it, it is readily available to everyone. . . . The holy name of Krishna is the controller of the opulence of liberation, and it is identical with Krishna. Simply by touching the holy name with one's tongue, immediate effects are produced. Chanting the holy name does not depend on initiation [or] pious activities. . . . The holy name does not wait for all these activities. It is self-sufficient" (29). These are extravagant words, but they cohere with the promise in "Awaiting On You All," that chanting the Lord's name will make one "free."

Chanting, however, is only one way to the Deity. If the right sort of sound can assist in bringing us closer to God, so can its seeming converse, silence.

2. The frequent failure of words to express feelings, especially love for another human being or love for God, is a regular theme in George's music. It appears, among other places, in "I Want To Tell You," "Learning How To Love You," "That Is All," "Never Get Over You," and "Mystical One." Sometimes words just aren't large enough for human experience, and we are reduced to silence. As George puts it in "What Is Life," "What I feel I can't say." Silence, however, is not an enemy to be shunned but, for the religious aspirant, a friend to be embraced, for silence can help conduct us to the Divine. "The Day The World Gets 'Round" approves of the minority who are seeking to make the world a better place. One of their attributes is that they engage in silent prayer. While no elaboration is offered, we learn more from "Pisces Fish." This song remarks that one can find "the Gods" only "in the deepest silence." This is a significant statement from a man who not only found chanting helpful but otherwise made his living by making musical noise.

For the most part, human beings exhibit a strong tendency to shun silence or stillness. We crave movement, sound, activity. Without them, we readily become bored. But George, following his religious teachers, knows that faith without silence is dead. This is not only because stillness is required for the important exercise of self-examination—something he promotes in "See Yourself"—but also because we often become aware of God only when normal activities cease: the divine presence prefers a sensory absence. We have spiritual senses as well as physical senses—one recalls the "spiritual eye" of "That's The Way It Goes"—and the former function best when the latter are temporarily shut down.

Both "Blow Away" and "Sat Singing" associate an experience of spiritual renewal with George's closing his eyes. He knows that feeling God may require temporarily abandoning, during prayer and meditation, the world of the five senses. Searching for God means sometimes declining to look at or listen to or think about the things that the material world thrusts before our faces. So darkness and stillness become George's spiritual collaborators, helping him to drag his attention away from this world of divertissement to the numinous world within his heart, where the neglected light of the Deity dwells. One recalls that, in the booklet for *Brainwashed*, the cartoon toward the end depicts George meditating with eyes shut.

So noise and light must go away. But outer silence and darkness must be mirrored by an inner silence and darkness. Internal sights and noises, just like external sights and noises, prevent us from divining the Reality within. So there must be a mental relaxation or letting go. Normal thinking must halt. Here the chief witness is "Sat Singing," George's record of an intense and overwhelming mystical experience. In this song he correlates achieving a higher consciousness with abandoning his everyday consciousness: "The moment that I lose my mind, you come into my heart." God has always been there, deep within George; but the singer's normal affairs have distracted him from perceiving this truth. So it's exchanging ordinary business for the inner hush of meditation that enables him to heed once again the divine knocking at the door of his heart.

3. The third practice that turns us away from the material world and toward God is the universal creative force we call love. This is indeed a central salvific concept for George, who sounds like a proponent of *bhakti* yoga. *Bhakti*, which derives from the Sanskrit root, "bhaj," meaning "be attached to" or "revere," is

intense spiritual devotion, the ineffable longing to love and be loved by God. Such mutual love is sacred, the highest emotion. For the devotee of *bhakti*, nothing except "unswerving devotion" (*Bhagavad-Gita* 11:54) really matters. The heart, in self-forgetfulness, passionately wants only one thing—God and God alone. Love, the virtue of virtues, is the ultimate discipline and the ultimate goal.

This is what George believes we should really be about. In "Sat Singing," the Divinity does not dispense practical wisdom or dole out doctrine or give advice on social issues. God instead simply says, "I'm always here for you to love." This is an invitation to George to "surrender," to give his self freely and in love to another. The divine love that flows through the universe calls forth love. It isn't a passive object but an active and longing subject. Like is calling to like.

Religious love is like human love: it grows as it is reciprocated. This is largely the meaning of "The Lord Loves The One (That Loves The Lord)." The song indeed correlates human and divine love in an almost mechanical way, as though God's love waits upon or is proportional to our love, as though it doesn't flow toward us unless love flows out from us toward God. But one needs to be careful here. As we shall see presently, the impression left by other compositions is that the ever-present God is gracious and works despite sizeable human failures.

Leaving that matter aside for the moment, "This Is Love" makes it plain that *bhakti*, the devotion of religious love, is the solution to the problem that is life: we can undo our troubles by using love, the "power" everyone has by nature. Now we saw in chapter 2 that, despite its centrality in his music and his thought, George doesn't explain love very well. As with chanting, he leaves us to ponder pretty much on our own. He neglects to define "love," and he doesn't explicate its relationship to worship or thanksgiving. He further often fails to unfold the practical implications of loving God, how it should, for instance, work itself out in our interpersonal relationships.

One fact, however, is perfectly clear. Whatever else love may be, it is for George a religious emotion, akin to romantic love. It is, in other words, above all some sort of feeling. In "My Sweet Lord" he ardently wants to love God "with more feeling." Elsewhere he characterizes his God with the emotionally charged words "sweet" ("My Sweet Lord") and "Dear" ("Dear One"). He indeed conceives of his God as being like a "lover" ("Your Love Is Forever," "Brainwashed")—a conceptualization which is so at home in Hinduism, above all in allegorical interpretations of the romantic love of Krishna and Radha. It's understandable that we often don't know whether George is singing about his wife or a girlfriend or God: he speaks to them and about them in much the same way.

What should be the spiritual outcome of love, along with silence and chanting? These devotional practices are intended to repair human hearts. If successful, they will uproot affection for the material world and in its place plant consciousness of the abiding divine presence. Attachment to God means detachment from the material world; and detachment from the material world means the extinguishing of desire; and the extinguishing of desire means the elimination of bad karma; and the elimination of bad karma means exiting the cycle of reincarnation and going on to a higher world. If we are to be saved, to be "free from birth" ("Give Me Love (Give Me Peace On Earth)") and avoid returning for yet another sad life in this inferior world, we must burn out our desire ("Hear Me Lord"). All of which is the teaching of the *Bhagavad-Gita:* "When the self is no longer attached to external objects, one finds the happiness that is in the Self. Such a one who is in union with God enjoys undying bliss" (5:21).

Having briefly reviewed some of the things George thinks we ought to do to be saved, I should like at this juncture to observe that he recognizes how hard it is to do what he enjoins. Harrisongs continually observe (contrary to Lennon's "All You Need Is Love") not that it's easy but that it's very hard. Faith demands much. After one hears the rumor of the reality of God, and even after the rumor has become reality in religious experience, human nature remains fond of the material world. The world's short-lived delights constantly beckon our attention, and despite knowing better, we give in and pay heed. We may have cleared the forests of falsehood and illusion, but as long as we are alive, they keep sprouting back up. The entirety of the CD *Brainwashed* is personal testimony to this miserable fact.[6]

"Rising Sun," for example, likens life to a room full of mirrors. For George the world is, even after decades of faith, confusing and deceptive. There are competing realities, and the one truth lies hidden among the many falsehoods. The upshot is that the ocean of love that flows on around us and within us is "easy . . . to miss." It's everywhere present and yet everywhere overlooked. Most of us never guess that the interior self conceals the vast, all-encompassing Deity and so carries within itself the answers to all of our deepest and most urgent questions. We've been "Brainwashed," forcibly indoctrinated with false beliefs and desires. Having eyes, we don't see; the presence of God remains camouflaged. Having ears, we don't hear; the still, small divine voice goes unnoticed. Paradoxically, we are "beggars in a goldmine" ("Dehra Dhun"), and enlightenment, which is nothing more than becoming who we already are, becomes arduous labor.

Maybe this is why George, in "Any Road," recounts how many things he has done far and wide. He tells us, for example, that he's gone into mountain caves and searched beneath the surface of the sea. What he seems to be saying is that the divine truth is not in the open or on the surface of things but hidden. So we are challenged to go hunting for it. We must become explorers, looking for a hidden, supraphysical land.

Changing metaphors, "Any Road" also informs us that we have to put up a good "fight." And the song indicates that it is precisely ourselves with whom we must do combat. This is because even the devout, to their constant frustration, always remain divided within themselves. The thoughts within us, as George explains, are both good and bad, darkness and light. We don't will one thing; our hearts are impure, of mixed motives. And even if we do "wake up" ("If You Believe," "Wake Up My Love"), we may soon enough go back to sleep. We need, then, to resolve to resist losing what we have gained ("That Which I Have Lost"). This entails, as "That's What It Takes" exhorts, that we must be "strong." Otherwise we're not going to get through the narrow gate that leads to the spiritual world. There are a million wide and easy zigzagging paths to reincarnating—"any road will take you there"—but only one narrow path toward escape and life, toward disentangling ourselves from this earthly realm and moving on to the blissful divine deep beyond. If we wish to possess the one thing needful, we must renounce everything that lies to the right and to the left; we must quit snatching at every passing thing that tickles our fancy and instead grope for God. "The resolute understanding is single; but the thoughts of the irresolute are many-branched and endless" (*Bhagavad-Gita* 2:41).

George once said: "I'm never going to get out of here unless it's by His grace, but then again, His grace is relative to the amount of desire I can manifest in myself. The amount of grace I would expect from God should be equal to the amount of grace I can gather or earn. I get out what I put in."[7] This remark, which makes God's presence both cause and effect, is consistent with "Writing's On The Wall," which tells us that our lives are in our hands, that our fate depends upon us, as well as with "Any Road," which teaches that we have to pay our "fare" for what we have bought. The "law of action"—the phrase George uses in "That Which I Have Lost"—requires that the measure we give will be the measure we get. The principle of reciprocity rules the spiritual life. Whatever we do will circle back to us. If we haven't given, we won't get back ("The Lord Loves The One (That Loves The Lord)"). Everything is on the karmic record ("Rising Sun"), and we won't get away without paying our debts ("Tears of the World," "Simply Shady").

Yet if we look at George's music as a whole, we also detect a strong belief in the efficacy of unmerited divine grace. The doctrine of karma is always there; and a song such as "Awaiting On You All" leaves the impression that God waits upon us, until we wake up and open our hearts. The same is true of "The Lord Loves The One (That Loves The Lord)." George, however, is honest enough about his own failings to acknowledge that he hasn't always kept up his end of the bargain, so in the end our singer knows that he's gotten more than he's put in.

Recall again "Rising Sun." In this we hear that God never let go of George's "umbilical cord." This last is a poetic way of referring to his spiritual lifeline. George had, in retrospect, become trapped, had indeed become a sort of amnesiac, forgetting the meaning of his life. God, however, never let loose of George. On the contrary, God graciously sent him a "messenger" from "inner space," and that's why George finally came to himself and remembered what he was here for. God in such a context is the abiding savior who never leaves or forsakes. Although George may have failed, the divine love remains steadfast. God faithfully continues to be an active participant in George's drama of salvation even when George has seemingly lost interest in the show.

George recounts another episode of grace in "That Which I Have Lost." In this little story, the singer requires help from someone else because he can't save himself. The light of his consciousness has grown dim, and so another needs to relight it and banish the darkness that has supplanted the light. And this is exactly what happens. When things became as bad as they can be, an inward light suddenly enters and brings renewal.

George's utter dependence upon divine grace, upon God as savior,[8] is also manifest in his recurrent prayers for help. In "Hear Me Lord," he pleads with God to give him more feelings of love. In "Give Me Love," George beseeches the Divinity to eliminate his karmic desire so that he will not have to reincarnate again. He repeatedly uses the word, "please." In "Living In The Material World," he reports that he prays to "the Spiritual Sky" so that he won't veer from his chosen religious course. In "Dear One," George addresses God directly with "move me toward Thee." George does not insist in any of these lines that God owes him. There is no bargaining. George simply prays words to his kind Lord, whom he hopes will answer him just because he's asked.

And then there's "Brainwashed." Most of this song addresses itself to those who are victims of the material world's propaganda and so mistakenly care about everything except God. Toward the end, however, George switches and addresses God directly. When he does, he asks God to lead us out of the "mess" we have fallen into: "Wish that you'd brainwash us too." It takes the creative hand of God to refashion the corrupted human race. Only God's grace saves us from and despite ourselves.

Throughout his music, George asks God to give him what he can't otherwise obtain on his own. God alone has the keys to open locked hearts. Only the Transcendent Self can make George transcend himself. And so it is that George prays; and when he prays, he expects the answer to come not because he has done this or that, but because of "the Lord Sri Krishna's grace."

Notes

1. Compare George Harrison, *I, Me, Mine* (San Francisco: Chronicle Books, 2002), 181: "our soul's desire is perfection."

2. Taken from a 1982 interview by Mukunda Goswami, available online at: www.krishna.org/Articles/2000/08/00066.html.

3. Harrison, *I, Me, Mine*, 158.

4. Ibid.

5. Note also his brief comments in ibid., 200, where he says that "Awaiting On You All" concerns Japa Yoga.

6. The personal nature of *Brainwashed* is rightly emphasized by Michael J. Gilmour, "Brainwashed, by George Harrison and the Bhagavad Gita," *Journal of Religion and Popular Culture* 8 (2004), available online at: www.usask.ca/relst/jrpc/art8-georgeharrison.html.

7. Taken from a 1982 interview by Mukunda Goswami, available online at: www.krishna.org/Articles/2000/08/00066.html.

8. On the need for religious saviors George was explicit; see Harrison, *I, Me, Mine*, 181. George also refers to saviors on "Tears Of The World."

Thanks for the Pepperoni

AN APPRECIATION

*I*t's easy to be a fan of George Harrison. He has left us with a series of beautiful songs that weather well in the memory. Some of these are known to almost everybody—"While My Guitar Gently Weeps," "Here Comes The Sun," "Something," "What Is Life," "Give Me Love (Give Me Peace On Earth)." Others are less well known but no less lovely and remain close to the hearts of those familiar with them—"Isn't It A Pity," "The Light That Has Lighted The World," "This Guitar Can't Keep From Crying," "Blow Away," "Tears Of The World," "Sat Singing," "That's The Way It Goes," "Cheer Down." George's musical corpus also contains some memorable performances with the slide guitar—"Sue Me, Sue You Blues" and "Marwa Blues" come immediately to mind—as well as a series of songs that are just plain fun to listen to—fun because they rock or make one smile. "Taxman," "Art Of Dying," "Awaiting On You All," "Living In The Material World," "This Song," "Crackerbox Palace," "Dream Away," "Devil's Radio," "P. 2 Vatican Blues," and "Brainwashed" are all examples. And then of course, beyond all of his own compositions, one can't forget how much George's accomplished guitar contributed to the sound of The Beatles.

George didn't consider himself a great lyricist, and in evaluating his music, one must admit that his poetic sensibilities were not supreme. His lyrics don't display Dylan's uncanny ability to mint memorable and quirky phrases. But what George often lacks in poetry or rhetoric, he makes up for with honesty. When he wants to praise his God, he does so, even if he thereby makes some of his listeners uneasy. And when he doesn't feel like praising his God, when in fact he feels lost or spiritually adrift, he lets us know, not pretending to be other than he is. He may be an evangelist, but he has nothing to hide, and so he registers his complaints. Such honesty is thoroughly admirable, and its source is obvious: George often sings not to us but to his God, and so we learn what's in his heart.

In addition to his honesty, I for one, despite being a Christian rather than a Hindu, appreciate George's infatuation with his God. Although George's eyes are wide open, so that he fully feels the woes of the world, he yet believes in a gracious God, who is the habitual center of his personal energy. This good God instructs him, inspires him, comforts him. And notwithstanding George's doubts, confusion, and sometime failure to feel God in his heart, his faith in his Deity endures, from the mid-sixties to his death in the new millennium. Through marital discord and musical disappointments, through religious fatigue and nearly being murdered, he remains persuaded that authentic meaning can only come from beyond, and that in the end all that matters is God.

This focus on God, the light that has enlightened George's life, leads to some disparagement of life in the material world, and this side of George may be harder for some to admire. But maybe that's because we typically see the world as the foreground with God as the background whereas for George it's the other way around; everything looks very different to him than it does to us. He may love the beauty of the natural world, and he may be passionate for humanitarian causes, but he fully realizes that, unlike God, all visible and material things must pass. They cannot, then, be of ultimate value.

The material world must also be relativized when one pays proper attention, as does George, to personal death and what lies beyond it. Of course, if death is the end, George must be wrong about everything. But if it is not, then he can be right about much. Certainly, if we ask ourselves where George is now and where we all will soon be, it's not this world. The products of our hands, including George's music, may live on here for a while, but what must matter to the dead, if anything still matters, is where they are now, somewhere beyond the material world. Preparing for that eventuality ahead of time, if it is real, seems to be wise and cannot but affect our appraisal of living in the material world. So even if George's stark distinction between what he calls in "Sat Singing" the "external world" and the inner world where the soul meets God seems sometimes overdone, in the end it is perhaps a helpful distortion, a sort of useful hyperbole in the cause of religious exhortation.

Finally, we should appreciate George's recurrent emphasis upon love. It's easy of course to be cynical here. It's one thing to sing, "All You Need Is Love" or "I Dig Love," another to explain what it means to love God and other people and to live accordingly. Nonetheless, compared to so much of today's popular music, with its rage and juvenile preoccupations, George's commendation of love, which gains content from his promulgation of humanitarian compassion and religious devotion, comes across as healthy and mature. It may sound quaint, but surely the world would not be a worse place if popular musicians more often invited us to pray to God to give us love and peace on earth.

The Songs of George Harrison

AN ANNOTATED LIST AND INDEX

- "All Things Must Pass." The song for which George's 1970 album is named. One can hear an acoustic demo on The Beatles' *Anthology 3* (1996), which was recorded during the 1969 *Get Back* sessions. Drawing generously from a poem in Timothy Leary's *Psychedelic Prayers after the Tao Te Ching* (Kerhonkson, NY: The Poets Press, 1966), George here reflects on the hard fact that everything we see and grasp passes away. This is why the rest of the album finds hope and meaning only in God, who does not pass away. See 37, 38, 62, 79, 85.
- "All Those Years Ago." This is the one hit—it reached number two in the U.S.—from *Somewhere In England* (1981). Although it's hardly one of George's best, it was popular because of the nostalgia that followed John Lennon's murder. Ringo Starr and Paul McCartney (and his wife Linda) joined the session. The song is confident in its affirmation of an afterlife and the importance of God but puzzling because of Lennon's uncertain connection with those two theological themes. Also strange is the discrepancy between the serious sentiments and the jaunty music; the tune was originally designed for lyrics about Ringo. A live version of the song appears on *Live In Japan* (1992). See 33, 52, 53, 80, 85, 88, 98, 101.
- "The Answer's At The End." This contribution to *Extra Texture: Read All About It* (1975) takes up words Sir Frank Crisp had inscribed on the walls of the mansion where George lived. The song expresses the

personal doubts and religious uncertainty George experienced in the mid-1970s. See 79, 84.

* "Any Road." The opening number to *Brainwashed* (2002). George had already done a live version in June 1997 on *Good Morning America* (when he was promoting Ravi Shankar's *Chants of India*). The song is a retrospective on life, especially on the difficulty of seeking and finding God. See 29, 50, 99, 101, 105, 109, 110, 128, 129.

* "Apple Scruffs." This song on *All Things Must Pass* (1970) takes up the nickname of the most rabid of Beatles fans, who waited for glimpses of the Fab Four outside of the Apple offices. At one time these devotees had their own publication, *Apple Scruff Monthly Magazine*. George allegedly took a particular fancy to one female among the Apple Scruffs, and she later recounted the details of her experiences in Carol Bedford, *Waiting for the Beatles: An Apple Scruff's Story* (Poole/Dorset: Blandford, 1985).

* "Art Of Dying." Although this warning to prepare for the inevitable first showed up on *All Things Must Pass* (1970), George had written it at least three years earlier. This impressive song teaches the difficulty of escaping the cycle of reincarnation. See 32, 79, 84, 86, 91, 118, 133, 157.

* "Awaiting On You All." According to *I, Me, Mine*, 200, this song on *All Things Must Pass* (1970) is about prayer beads and mantras. It also expresses George's syncretistic view of Jesus and his conviction that religion is in the heart, not in institutions. The *The Concert For Bangladesh* (1971) offers a live version. See 29, 32, 42, 47, 49, 55, 58, 67, 124, 129, 131n.5, 133.

* "Baby Don't Run Away." A repetitious and to my mind irritating love song on *Gone Troppo* (1982). It's one of the reasons the album didn't sell well.

* "Badge." George wrote this with Eric Clapton, and Cream recorded it for *Goodbye* (1969). The chorus of "Badge" was part of the inspiration for George's "Here Comes The Sun," and its lyrics are typically George in that they remark upon opposites ("up and down") and the cyclical nature of things ("the wheel goes 'round").

* "Ballad Of Sir Frankie Crisp (Let It Roll)." A song for the eccentric nineteenth-century baron and builder of George's beloved mansion, on *All Things Must Pass* (1970). See 63.

- "Baltimore Oriole." George's version of an old Hoagie Carmichael favorite, on *Somewhere In England* (1981).
- "Bangla Desh." This plea for humanitarian assistance was first released as a single. A live version can be found on *The Concert For Bangladesh* (1971). See 69, 140.
- "Be Here Now." This takes its title from Ram Das's book of the same name (1971). It's on *Living In The Material World* (1973), and anticipates two of George's later songs, "Just For Today" and "The Flying Hour." Being "here now" means, for George, no longer living in his past as a Beatle. See 84, 85, 115, 142, 148.
- "Beautiful Girl." A love song for Olivia on *Thirty-Three & 1/3* (1976), with effective vocals.
- "Behind That Locked Door." Some country and western advice and encouragement for Bob Dylan, on *All Things Must Pass* (1970).
- "Between The Devil And The Deep Blue Sea." The only cover on *Brainwashed* (2002). George had already played this Harold Arlen/Ted Koehler classic live in 1992, for a British Channel 4 documentary, *Mister Roadrunner*.
- "Beware Of Darkness." A rumination on the Indian concept of *maya* or illusion, on *All Things Must Pass* (1970). The song serves as a warning: Don't unconsciously pursue the vanities of the material world. *The Concert For Bangladesh* (1971) contains a live version, and an old demo, with incomplete lyrics, is on the remastered *All Things Must Pass* (2001). See 32, 34, 63, 66, 100.
- "Bhajahu Re Mana." An eight-minute number on *Chant And Be Happy* (1991).
- "Bhaja Bhakata/Arati." Another eight-minute number on *Chant And Be Happy* (1991).
- "A Bit More Of You." A short instrumental on *Extra Texture: Read All About It* (1975) which reprises the opening song of the album, "You." It's filler.
- "Blood From A Clone." The opening song on *Somewhere In England* (1981) was written and recorded only after Mo Ostin—to whom the earlier "Mo" is a tribute—had rejected the album George had submitted to him. It's firstly a testament to George's anger at the record industry. See 98.

- "Blow Away." This was the one big hit on *George Harrison* (1979). It's a beautiful record of George's optimism. He attributed its origin to belief in what his Hindu masters taught him, that human beings are potentially divine. The "you" seems to be God. See further Harrison, *I, Me, Mine*, 378; also above, 12, 18, 71, 83, 90, 103, 125, 132.
- "Blue Jay Way." George tells the insubstantial story behind this dreary song, which was on *Magical Mystery Tour* (1967), in *I, Me, Mine*, 114.
- "Brainwashed." The catchy, grand finale to *Brainwashed* (2002) and to George's career. Here he once again becomes the preacher, and the explicit religious sentiments sound more like the George of the seventies than the George of the eighties or nineties. Some critics disliked the obvious targets—big business, big government, big education—but the religiosity is sincere, the music rollicking and effective. See 6, 7, 29, 48, 56, 66, 67, 72, 85, 90, 99, 101, 102, 108, 111, 120, 123, 127,130, 133.
- "Breath Away From Heaven." This poetically polished love song is on *Cloud Nine* (1987). It was initially on the soundtrack to the movie *Shanghai Surprise*.
- "Bye Bye, Love." This entry to *Dark Horse* (1974) is George's satiric rewrite of the Everly Brothers' 1957 classic (written by Felice and Boudleaux Bryant). It's testimony to George's failed marriage to Pattie Boyd and her moving on to Eric Clapton (here referred to as "old Clapper"). For the final mix, Pattie sang and Clapton played guitar!
- "(Can Only) Run So Far." First written for Eric Clapton, it appears on his *Journeyman* (1989). George used it on *Brainwashed* (2002). It's about the emptiness of life as a rock-and-roll star. See 116.
- "Can't Stop Thinking About You." A typical, mid-seventies pop love song on *Extra Texture: Read All About It* (1975). Obviously written to be a hit, it contains no theology. Some of the critical reviewers signaled it out as a highlight of the album; others found it boring.
- "Cheer Down." Written with Tom Petty for the soundtrack of *Lethal Weapon 2*, he put it on *The Best Of Dark Horse* (1989). A live, infectious version is available on *Live In Japan* (1992). "Cheer down" is reportedly what Oliva would say to George when he was getting manic. See 132.

* "Circles." The conclusion to *Gone Troppo* (1982), this song views all of life as circular and offers a clear statement of reincarnation. See 80, 82.
* "Cloud Nine." According to George, the artwork on the cover of *Cloud Nine* (1987), encouraged him to make this song the name of the album. The Temptations, in 1969, had a song and an album by that title, and George's tune recalls it at several points. *Live In Japan* (1992) offers an alternative and in some ways superior version. If there is any religious message, it remains opaque. What matters here is the guitar work.
* "Cockamamie Business." An autobiographical reflection, only on *The Best Of Dark Horse* (1989). The lyrics meander, from Ed Sullivan to Bad Company to the environment to women to the record business to taxes. See 70, 76, 116.
* "Cosmic Empire." Recorded during or around the time of the *All Things Must Pass* (1970) sessions. George never used or went back to this happy song, and it is known only through bootlegs. The refrain is, "Down at the cosmic empire." The song obviously expresses a religious worldview and sets forth a religious goal, but the words—some of which are indistinct on the bootlegs—remain cryptic.
* "Cowboy Music." An instrumental piece on *Wonderwall* (1968).
* "Crackerbox Palace." The one hit from *Thirty-Three & 1/3* (1976), it reached number nineteen on the Billboard chart. George has a helpful account of this song in *I, Me, Mine*, 334. He there says that, in his mind, the song can be taken to be about life in general. The amusing music video version is on *The Dark Horse Years 1976–1992* (2004). See 29, 34, 39n.11, 80, 133.
* "Cry For A Shadow." A parody instrumental written in 1961 with John Lennon, it appeared on The Beatles *Anthology 1* (1995). See 35.
* "Crying." An instrumental on *Wonderwall* (1968).
* "Dark Horse." This gave its name to George's 1974 album. His comments in *I, Me, Mine*, 288, are a bit obscure, as are the lyrics. Is George singing to his ex about adultery, or is he telling his critics that his public image doesn't correspond to reality? Religious themes are absent. The song would probably have gone higher than the fifteenth slot on the Billboard chart if George's voice had not been wrecked by laryngitis. He himself thought that he sounds like

Louis Armstrong on this one. The song is also on *Live In Japan* (1992). On the story behind the Dark Horse symbol itself, which George first saw on the side of a tin container in India, one may now consult the little book that accompanies the boxed set, *The Dark Horse Years 1976–1992*.

* "Dark Sweet Lady." A love song to George's wife, Olivia, on *George Harrison* (1979). See 12.
* "The Day The World Gets 'Round." A sad glance back at the broken utopian dreams of the 1960s. George mourns how few are working for a better world and paying homage to God. It's on *Living In The Material World* (1973). See 22, 33, 37, 56, 69, 124.
* "Dear One." A happy love song to God on *Thirty-Three & 1/3* (1976). It reflects a religious renewal following the melancholy of *Extra Texture: Read All About It*. It was written for Paramhansa Yogananda, author of *Autobiography of a Yogi*, one of George's favorite books. See 8, 12, 49, 74, 127, 130.
* "Deep Blue." This was the B-side for the "Bangla Desh" single (1971). Although it never received much notice and has now been almost forgotten, it's George's musically beautiful and lyrically moving response to his mother's death from cancer. It's a prayer to God for help, light, love, and understanding in the midst of personal grief. See 90.
* "Dehra Dhun." Dehra Dhun is a village in India. In *The Beatles Anthology* DVD, George, when reminiscing about The Beatles' time in India in 1968, recalls this song and plays some of it. He recorded more than one version of it in 1969–1970, which neither he nor The Beatles ever released, perhaps because the song is so repetitious. It's only available on bootlegs. See 128.
* "Devil's Radio." A fun rocker on *Cloud Nine* (1987). It's not just about gossip but *māya*, illusion. *Live In Japan* (1992) has a live version. See 96–97, 100–101, 133, 145.
* "Ding Dong, Ding Dong." A lyrically simple celebration of New Year's whose introductory chimes seem to be a variation of Big Ben's bells. The words were taken mostly from an inscription at the Harrison mansion. George expected this song from *Dark Horse* (1974) to be a big holiday hit. It wasn't.

- "Don't Bother Me." This was George's first real composition for The Beatles and it appeared on *With The Beatles* (1963) in the U.K., on *Meet The Beatles* (1964) in the U.S. See 35.
- "Don't Let Me Wait Too Long." A secular love song on *Living In The Material World* (1973). It might have been a hit had it been released as a single.
- "Dream Away." The delightful theme song to the equally delightful film *Time Bandits*. The song, which appears on *Gone Troppo* (1982), features the juxtaposition of opposites and observes the dreamlike quality of existence, both standard Harrison themes. The chorus—"Oh ry in ey ay," etc.—appears to be nonsense. See 65, 83, 84, 133.
- "Dream Scene." An instrumental piece on *Wonderwall* (1968).
- "Drilling A Home." Another instrumental piece on *Wonderwall* (1968).
- "End Of The Line." One of George's offerings for *The Traveling Wilburys, Vol. 1* (1988). Although the song is lighthearted, one wonders whether the repeated line, "it's all right," isn't for George a cosmic statement: all is well and all will be well, with everybody.
- "Fantasy Sequins." An instrumental on *Wonderwall* (1968).
- "Far East Man." George wrote this entrée for *Dark Horse* (1974) with assistance from The Rolling Stones' Ronnie Wood, who put his own version (with Harrison in the background) on *I've Got My Own Album To Do* (1974). The song expresses George's humanitarian impulse, his regrets about the world's current state, his faint utopian hope for something better, and the importance of following one's own heart. See 15, 34, 69, 73.
- "Faster." George released this as a single as well as on the album, *George Harrison* (1979). It's about the fame of a Grand Prix race driver, the title being taken from Jackie Stewart's autobiography. George believed that the lyrics also had something to say about fame in general. The video, which features Stewart, is on the DVD for *The Dark Horse Years 1976–1992* (2004). See 102.
- "Fish On The Sand." On this number for *Cloud Nine* (1987), George meditates on the distance between his theology and his experience. His religious feelings are frustrated, but he knows that, without God, he's nothing but a "Fish On The Sand." Like "Pisces Fish," this

THE LOVE THERE THAT'S SLEEPING

reveals that George paid attention to his astrological sign. See 9, 10, 15, 20, 74.

- "Flying Hour." Written with Mick Relphs, the lyrics recall "Be Here Now," but most of the words are taken from a saying of Frank Crisp, the former owner of George's estate: "Past is gone, thou canst not that recall. Future is not, may not be at all. Present is, improve the flying hour. Present only is within thy power." The song is available on *Songs By George Harrison* (1989) and, much more easily, on bootlegs. See 85.
- "For You Blue." Written for *Let It Be* (1970), it's also on *The Best Of George Harrison* (1976). George did a live version of this charming love song on his 1974 tour.
- "Gat Kirwani." An instrumental for *Wonderwall* (1968).
- "Give Me Love (Give Me Peace On Earth)." A number one hit and the opening song to *Living In The Material World* (1973). It's a musically beautiful and lyrically simple prayer both for the idealistic dreams of the 1960s—peace and love—as well as for George's religious ambitions—divine light and freedom from reincarnation. Both times, after the main two verses, we hear "OM." George did the song for his *Live In Japan* (1992) tour. See 22, 34, 79, 82, 90, 116, 122, 127, 130, 132, 150.
- "Glass Box." An instrumental piece on *Wonderwall* (1968).
- "Going Down To Golders Green." Recorded during or around the time of the *All Things Must Pass* (1970) sessions, it was left in the can and survives only on bootlegs. George sounds as though he's trying to imitate, in turn, Elvis Presley, Carl Perkins, and Roy Orbison.
- "Gone Troppo." The title track for his poorly received 1982 album, this is a carefree celebration of the tropical life George enjoyed when he was staying, as he did often, at his Hawaiian home in Hana, Maui. The expression, "gone troppo," is generally taken to refer to leaving western civilization for a prolonged or permanent stay in the tropics, but it is also Australian slang for going crazy. See 710.
- "Gopala Krishna." A pleasing song about Krishna in his famous form as a cowherd. George evidently recorded this in 1969 (during the sessions that produced the "Hare Krishna Mantra") and/or 1970 (during the *All Things Must Pass* sessions) but never released it. One can hear it on bootlegs.

* "Got My Mind Set on You." George's hit remake—it reached number one in the U.S., number two in Britain—of an old number written by Rudy Clark and performed by James Ray (1962). George first heard it in 1963. It's on *Cloud Nine* (1987) as well as *Live In Japan* (1992). There are also two video versions in circulation; both are silly, and both are included in the DVD for *The Dark Horse Years 1976–1992* (2004). See 9, 57, 117, 148.
* "Govinda." The opening song on *Chant And Be Happy* (1991). "Govinda" is one of the names of Krishna. Moreover, according to Hindu lore, "Govinda" is the name of the world's earliest poem, composed by Brahma, the first mortal. When first released in 1970, the single charted in Britain. The Hare Krishnas have used it in religious ritual. The lead guitar is George's.
* "Govinda Jaya Jaya." This is a highly repetitious chant that lasts ten minutes and winds up *Chant And Be Happy* (1991).
* "Greasy Legs." An instrumental piece on *Wonderwall* (1968).
* "Greece." Although the album cover of *Gone Troppo* (1982) lists this catchy number as an instrumental, one can hear George softly singing; but what he's saying, apart from "Greece," is terribly hard to make out.
* "Grey Cloudy Lies." A profoundly depressing meditation on despair and suicide from *Extra Texture: Read All About It* (1975). One has trouble imagining anyone enjoying it. See 7.
* "Guru Vandana." An instrumental piece on *Wonderwall* (1968). The Guru Vandana is a ten-line Hindu chant in honor of God and one's teacher. It contains two common idioms that reappear in Harrisongs. "I bow to the lotus feet of my guru" has its parallel in "Stuck Inside A Cloud," where George expresses his desire to touch the "lotus feet" of his master or God; and "rubs the dirt off the mirror of the devotee's heart" reminds one of "That Which I Have Lost," where the "dust" on the "mirrors" of the understanding needs to be removed.
* "Handle With Care." Successfully released as a single, this is on *The Traveling Wilburys, Vol. 1* (1988). Although most of the Wilburys' songs were joint efforts, the U.K. copyright for this one belongs to George. We know that George at least came up with the title (he took it from a box that happened to be lying around) and that he

penned the stanza that begins with "I'm so tired of being lonely" for Roy Orbison to sing.

* "Hare Krishna Mantra." George sang on and produced this 1969 version of the Hare Krishnas' main chant. It charted as a single, making its way to number one in West Germany and Czechoslovakia and into the top ten almost everywhere else in Europe then reappeared years later on *Chant And Be Happy* (1991). See 46, 122, 153.
* "Hari's On Tour" is the repetitious instrumental introduction to *Dark Horse* (1974). A live version from George's 1974 appearance in Washington, D.C., is on *Songs By George Harrison: Volume Two* (1992).
* "Headed For The Light." A buoyant, confident anticipation of death and the life beyond; it's on *The Traveling Wilburys, Vol. 1* (1988). See 18, 19, 20, 75, 80, 88, 108, 116.
* "Hear Me Lord." A completely sincere and self-revealing plea for divine forgiveness on *All Things Must Pass* (1970). As George cries out, "forgive me," "help me," "hear me," one feels his utter, childlike dependence upon God. See 84, 108, 111, 127, 130.
* "Here Comes The Moon." Written when George was on LSD or mushrooms in the late 1970s, this is an obvious companion piece to his earlier and much better "Here Comes The Sun." Written in response to a spectacular sunset in Hawaii, it appears on *George Harrison* (1979). The lyrics convey infatuation with the natural world, here interpreted as "God's gift." The recent CD of *George Harrison* contains a demo version. See 82, 90.
* "Here Comes The Sun." Written (reportedly in Eric Clapton's garden) after a bad patch having to do with The Beatles' finances, it's a straightforward articulation of joy. Both the *Concert For Bangladesh* (1971) and *Live In Japan* (1992) contain live versions of this, deservedly one of George's best-loved songs. The former is acoustic, the latter electric. It first appeared on *Abbey Road* (1969). See 10, 38, 88, 90, 112, 132.
* "His Name Is Legs (Ladies & Gentlemen)." This is about an eccentric friend of George, Legs Larry Smith. It's on *Extra Texture: Read All About It* (1975) and can have no meaning beyond George's circle of friends, who have spoken of Smith as George's private jester. Smith is an artist and did the delightful cover art for *Gone Troppo*.

- "The Hold Up." Written with then session musician David Bromberg, this was released on Bromberg's 1972 self-titled album. The theme is the same as "Taxman."
- "Hong Kong Blues." One of two Hoagy Carmichael remakes for *Somewhere In England* (1981), the other being "Baltimore Oriole." George remembered listening when he was a young child to "Hong Kong Blues" on the radio.
- "Horse To Water." This appears on *Jools Holland's "Small World, Big Band"* (2001). George's last song, he finished the vocals only weeks before he died and only weeks before the album appeared. The song promotes "God realization," rejects Christian fundamentalism, and articulate sadness about a friend who drinks too much. See 54, 100, 120.
- "Hottest Gong In Town." Written for the soundtrack of *Shanghai Surprise*, this is hard to come by, being available only on bootlegs and the expensive collector's book, *Songs By George Harrison: Volume 2* (1992).
- "I'd Have You Anytime." Dylan cowrote this piece for *All Things Must Pass* (1970). The story is in Harrison, *I, Me, Mine*, 164.
- "I Dig Love." The most shallow contribution to *All Things Must Pass* (1970), this laid-back number, which has a druggy feel, appears to be little more than a thoughtless endorsement of the free love movement of the late 1960s. See 134.
- "I Don't Care Anymore." This, the nadir of George's musical corpus, was the forgettable flipside to the single, "Ding Dong, Ding Dong." The singer begins by announcing that he needs a B-side number. One can't take him very seriously after that, and thank goodness. The lyrics, which wantonly defend an adulterous relationship, must be condemned, to borrow from "Devil's Radio," as "words that thoughtless speak." This is not what we need to hear from anybody.
- "I Don't Want To Do It." A forgotten Dylan piece that George worked on more than once, beginning in 1970 or so. One version finally showed up in, of all places, the soundtrack to *Porky's Revenge* (1985). Today it's easy to find it on bootlegs.
- "I Live For You." Recorded for the original *All Things Must Pass* (1970), this touching confession, with its country twang, which manages to convey hope and melancholy at the same time, didn't

THE LOVE THERE THAT'S SLEEPING

make the final cut. It appeared only on the remastered thirtieth anniversary reissue CD (2001). One might, if not well acquainted with George, take the words to concern a woman, but they don't. The song is about George's being alone and sad and yet not falling into despair because he cares not for the world but for the God he can feel inside him. Nothing else matters because George lives for God. See 26, 31, 34, 64, 89, 118.

- "I Me Mine." George took the title of this song, which first appeared on *Let It Be* (1970), for his autobiography. For him it is a religious statement of the dangers of egoism. It was the last song The Beatles ever did together, and was recorded long after the other pieces for the album had already been done.
- "I Need You." A warmhearted love song that is one of the highlights of The Beatles' *Help!* (1965).
- "I Really Love You." George's homage to doo-wop, this is a cover of the 1961 hit written by Leroy Swearingen and performed by The Stereos. It's on *Gone Troppo* (1982).
- "I Remember Jeep." An instrumental jam session on *All Things Must Pass* (1970) that, at eight minutes and with much repetition, goes on too long.
- "I Want To Tell You." Written for *Revolver* (1966), this is one of several songs in which George stresses the limitations of words. He redid it for *Live In Japan* (1992). See 124.
- "If I Needed Someone." The lyrics of this number, written for *Rubber Soul* (1965), are uninteresting. *Live In Japan* (1992) has a version of the song.
- "If Not For You." George covered this Dylan tune for *All Things Must Pass* (1970) and reprised it, with a particularly nice slide effort, for the 1992 Madison Square Garden celebration of Dylan's music, although it didn't make the official album for the event (and so one has to go to bootlegs to hear it). One wonders whether George didn't think about God when singing it.
- "If You Believe." Written with Gary Wright, this musically derivative but lyrically interesting contribution to *George Harrison* (1979) appears to rework several New Testament verses. It exhorts listeners not only to believe but also to pray. See 11, 57, 121, 122, 128.

- "I'll Still Love You (When Every Song Is Sung)." George wrote this when he was working on *All Things Must Pass* (1970) but it appeared on *Ringo's Rotogravure* (1976). When Ringo sang it, he was presumably thinking about a woman. When George wrote it, he may have been reflecting on God. See 37.
- "In My Life." George performed this Lennon-McCartney classic on his 1974 Dark Horse tour. Instead of singing, "in my life I love you more," George sang: "in my life I love God more." See 81.
- "In Spite Of All The Danger." A 1958 song written with Paul but sung by John. It can be heard on The Beatles *Anthology 1* (1995).
- "In The Park." A *Wonderwall* (1968) instrumental.
- "The Inner Light." The B-side of "Lady Madonna" (1968) which later appeared on The Beatles' *Rarities* (1978) and *Past Masters: Volume Two* (1988). The perfect song for reflective introverts, it's based upon a passage in the *Tao Te Ching*. See 26, 27, 38n.2, 90.
- "Isn't It A Pity." A beautiful, haunting lament for broken relationships, with George pointing the finger of guilt at himself. Originally on *All Things Must Pass* (1970), in two different versions, it was performed on George's Japanese tour and so appears on *Live In Japan* (1992). There's also another live version on *The Concert For Bangladesh* (1971). See 34, 96, 132.
- "It Don't Come Easy." Recorded in 1970, this was a big hit for Ringo in 1971. It was the product of collaboration with George, who produced and played the guitar. How much the latter contributed is unknown. There is a bootleg of a studio take, without the horns, in which George, not Ringo, is the vocalist. Was George supplying a guide vocal for Ringo to follow? In this version one can plainly hear, at 1:41 into the song, "Hare Krishna." The two words are buried almost beyond hearing in Ringo's version.
- "It Is 'He' (Jai Sri Krishna)." George recovered his enthusiasm for chanting during a trip to India in 1973; this song on *Dark Horse* (1974) was the result.
- "It's All Too Much." This showed up on The Beatles' *Yellow Submarine* (1969) after being recorded in 1967 and cut from *Magical Mystery Tour*. Although on the surface this seems to be nothing but a conventional love song, one can perhaps already detect George's

THE LOVE THERE THAT'S SLEEPING

emerging religious worldview when he sings, "I'm everywhere," and refers to "a love that's shining all around."

- "It's Johnny's Birthday." An instrumental on *All Things Must Pass* (1970), based upon Cliff Richards's 1968 version of "Congratulations," a song written by Bill Martin and Phil Coulter. The "Johnny" is John Lennon, not John Barham, who did the orchestral arrangements for *All Things Must Pass*.

- "It's What You Value." For the story behind this see Harrison, *I, Me, Mine*, 322. While the title is promising, the lyrics don't say much and are less interesting than the pleasing melody. It's on *Thirty-Three & 1/3* (1976).

- "Just For Today." At his February 1988 Toronto press conference to promote *Cloud Nine*, George said this: "I had these three friends who were all in AA at my house one night back in 1983, and this guy showed me a brochure that was called 'Just For Today.' It seemed so nice, you know, a nice idea, to try and live through this day only. I mean, it's not just for alcoholism. It's good for everybody to remember that we can only live today and the only thing that really exists is now. The past is gone, the future we don't know about. So it's like an extension of the 'Be Here Now' idea. I thought it would make a nice song, so I wrote it. But it's good also for AA, I think. Maybe we could make it into a TV commercial." See 100.

- "Lay His Head." This B-side to "Got My Mind Set On You" also appears on *Songs By George Harrison* (1989) and bootlegs. Taking up a saying of Jesus from the New Testament, George here feels trapped by his fame while he longs for love, perhaps God's love as well as a woman's love. See 57, 117.

- "Learning How To Love You." Written originally for Herb Albert, who didn't use it, this love ballad showed up on *Thirty-Three & 1/3* (1976). See 124.

- "Let It Down." One of the several love songs on *All Things Must Pass* (1970). There is an alternative mix on the 2001 remastered *All Things Must Pass*.

- "Life Itself." A love song to God on *Somewhere In England* (1981). It amounts to a series of theological assertions: God sends the gifts of the natural world; God is "the truth"; God is "life itself"; God is love; God is reality; God is the one who meets us in death; God is a friend; and God is known by many names, among them Christ, Vishnu, and Buddha. *Songs By George Harrison: Volume 2* (1992) contains a demo. See 8, 12, 18, 55, 74, 80, 88.

* "The Light That Has Lighted The World." George almost named the album *Living In The Material World* (1973) after this entrée. The beautiful song expresses resentment toward those who dislike the ex-Beatle George but thanksgiving for those who reflect the light of God. See 22, 90, 97, 132.

* "Living In The Material World." Musically powerful, this is the title track for George's 1973 album. It reflects his dualistic anthropology, recalls his time as a Beatle (here disparaged), warns that one can never gratify the senses, expresses George's prophetic self-consciousness, conveys his desire to quit this world, and declares his belief in salvation through Krishna's grace. See 25, 61, 63, 64, 67, 74, 79, 130, 133.

* "Long, Long, Long." The "you" on this simple love song is God. We know this from George's comments, not the lyrics themselves, which are cryptic. It's on *The Beatles (The White Album)* (1968).

* "Looking For My Life." This appears to be George's response to the attack upon his life in 1999. Appearing on *Brainwashed* (2002), it effectively communicates his stunned surprise and also seems to preserve his conviction that, when death was close at hand, he was not wholly happy with his preparation for it. See 11, 21, 80, 81, 109, 110, 111, 153.

* "The Lord Loves The One (That Loves the Lord)." In accord with the rest of the entries on *Living In The Material World* (1973), this song preaches karma, warns about judgment at death, and exalts love as our most important aspiration. See 45, 79, 85, 86, 126, 129.

* "Love Comes To Everyone." This is the optimistic opening for *George Harrison* (1979). Although one could perchance give it a nonreligious reading, as though it were about human love, George is singing about a love inside the heart that neither ages nor changes, by which he means God's love. Near the end he borrows religious language from the New Testament (Matthew 7:7 and Luke 11:9). Although the song was released as a single, it sadly never became popular. See 12, 28, 56.

- "Love Scene." An instrumental on *Wonderwall* (1968).
- "Love You To." A Beatles' song from 1966, on *Revolver*. The sitar is central here, and George is already warning us about filling ourselves up with the things we can see with our eyes. See 44.
- "Marwa Blues." An instrumental for *Brainwashed* (2002). This simple and relaxing guitar piece won an Emmy for "Best Pop Instrumental Performance" in 2004. See 2, 132.
- "Maxine." A demo rejected for *The Traveling Wilburys, Vol. 3* (1990). It's available on bootlegs. The words, which raise the possibility that Maxine has been abducted by a flying saucer, are pure fun; there's no message here.
- "Maya Love." Like other songs on *Dark Horse* (1974), this slide number derives from the dissolution of George's first marriage. In this context, *"mâya"* means the illusory nature of sensible things. See 64, 65.
- "Microbes." An instrumental piece on *Wonderwall* (1968).
- "Miss O'Dell." This is the B-side of the hit single, "Give Me Love (Give Me Peace On Earth)" (1973), rightly considered not good enough for *Living In The Material World*. One can find it now only on bootlegs. It's a throwaway; George frequently breaks out laughing. The story behind the song is in *I, Me, Mine*, 248. See 116.
- "Mo." Written in 1977 to honor the fiftieth birthday of Warner Brother's Mo Ostin, it didn't appear on a record until a six-box CD (*Mo's Blues*) was released to commemorate Ostin's retirement as Chief Executive in 1994. As only 600 copies of the set were produced, most of us know "Mo" only through bootlegs. There is some nice guitar work on this affectionate and lyrically lightweight song, which toward the end has George saying, "reaping what you sow." If "Mo" had different words and had been released as a single, it might have been a hit. See 57, 137.
- "My Sweet Lord." The big number one single from *All Things Must Pass* (1970), which climbed to the top place once again on the British charts shortly after George's death in 2001. Two live versions of this exist, one on the *The Concert For Bangladesh* (1971), the other on *Live In Japan* (1992). There is also a new but inferior version on the remastered *All Things Must Pass* (2001). *I, Me, Mine*, 176, gives us George's exegesis of this song, which intentionally mixes Hindu

and Christian elements. See 2, 6, 7, 21, 36, 46, 55, 122, 127, 157, 160.

* "Mystical One." This contribution to *Gone Troppo* (1982) is a clear statement of George's love for God as well as a reflection of his up-and-down religious experience. The reissued CD features a demo version. See 95, 121, 124.

* "Never Get Over You." A love song, presumably for Olivia, on *Brainwashed* (2002). See 124.

* "Nobody's Child." A cover of a song written by Mel Foree and Cy Coben. The post-Orbison Wilburys did it, at George's instigation, for *Nobody's Child: Romanian Angel Appeal* (1990). There are bootlegs of The Beatles singing this in Hamburg in 1961. The version for the Romanian cause has a new stanza from George, making the song relevant for that humanitarian crisis.

* "No Time Or Space." Born of infatuation with the electronic synthesizer, then new, this is the second side of *Electronic Sound* (1969, released by Zapple, an experimental division of Apple). It should have been called *Electronic Noise*. Surely no one ever listened to it more than once. Happily, George knew better than to try this sort of thing again.

* "Not Guilty." Although this was not released until *George Harrison* (1979), it was written in 1968, for the *White Album* sessions, and it reflects his conflict with the other Beatles. Here he is unapologetic about his own religious commitment and about getting John, Paul, and Ringo involved in Hinduism. The Beatles recorded the song and didn't use it until it showed up on *Anthology 3* (1996). See 112n.1.

* "Old Brown Shoe." The B-side of "The Ballad Of John And Yoko" (1969), this also showed up on The Beatles' *Hey Jude* (1970). *Live In Japan* (1992) has a nice version, and The Beatles' *Anthology 3* (1996) preserves an interesting demo. It has no religious import, although it does reflect George's preoccupation with dualities and contradictions (right and wrong, short and long, up and down, etc.).

* "On The Bed." An instrumental piece on *Wonderwall* (1968).

* "Only A Northern Song." An outtake from *Sgt. Pepper's* that appeared on The Beatles' *Yellow Submarine* (1969). *I, Me, Mine*, 100, characterizes the song as a "joke" about Liverpool. See 31.

- "Ooh Baby (You Know That I Love You)." A love song on *Extra Texture: Read All About It* (1975), written in imitation of Smokey Robinson's style. See 12.
- "Out Of The Blue." The most subdued instrumental jam on *All Things Must Pass* (1970). The overextended eleven-minute track has a jazzy feel to it, with saxophones and guitar lines exchanging the lead throughout.
- "P. 2 Vatican Blues (Last Saturday Night)." A jaunty outtake from *Cloud Nine* that later showed up on *Brainwashed* (2002). The prefatory "P. 2" in the title, written in George's own hand in the CD booklet, may mean nothing more than that the lyrics to the song belong on page 2 of that booklet. The whole song reflects George's antipathy for organized Roman Catholicism. The reference to "white smoke" has nothing to do with George's cigarette habit but rather refers to the ritual surrounding the selection of a new Pope by the College of Cardinals. Also, although some have connected mention of a "concrete tuxedo" with George's expectation of death, this is unlikely given the date of the original composition. See 41, 42, 99, 133.
- "Party Seacombe." An instrumental piece on *Wonderwall* (1968).
- "Photograph." George wrote this sentimental number with Ringo, for whom it was a big hit. In 1973 it was released as a single and on *Ringo*. Ringo chose to sing this in honor of George for the "Concert For George."
- "Piggies." One of George's contributions to *The Beatles (The White Album)* (1968), this is an ungenerous satire on the British upper class. There is a live version on *Live In Japan* (1992) and a demo on The Beatles' *Anthology 3* (1996). See 72, 97, 98.
- "Pisces Fish." A serious meditation on George as a Pisces, found on *Brainwashed* (2002). The song successfully communicates the distance the alienated singer feels between the external world and the divine life that flows within him. See 25, 27, 50, 70, 80, 82, 86, 89, 90, 101, 109, 124, 141, 153.
- "Plug Me In." A loud and disorderly three-minute instrumental jam session on *All Things Must Pass* (1970). The raucous drumbeat and imposing piano bass lines almost drown out the bluesy guitar leads.
- "Poor Little Girl." Only on *The Best of Dark Horse* (1989), this meditation contrasts young people who are looking for transient physical

love with the search to understand true love, that is, divine love. See 74, 118.
* "Prayers To A Spiritual Master." This was the B-side of the single "The Hare Krishna Mantra."
* "Pure Smokey." A prayer of thanks to God for the music of Smokey Robinson, on *Thirty-Three & 1/3* (1976). See 190.
* "Red Lady Too." An instrumental for *Wonderwall* (1968).
* "Ride Rajbun." Written with David English, George did this song for a TV cartoon series, *The Bunbury Tales*. A soundtrack was released (1992), but "Ride Rajbun" is hard to hear because it is background for a narrator.
* "Rising Sun." This follows "Pisces Fish" and "Looking For My Life" on *Brainwashed* (2002) and amplifies themes found in them—the divine life is within and George was inadequately prepared for death when it came to him. See 18, 20, 30, 44, 86, 99, 101, 110, 128, 129.
* "Rocking Chair In Hawaii." A contribution to *Brainwashed* (2002) that developed from a 1970 demo entitled, "Down To The River." The love song is notable for its two mentions of Sai Baba, although the song doesn't have any religious meaning. See 11.
* "Roll Over Beethoven." George sang this Chuck Berry hit for *With The Beatles* (1963) and thirty years later reprised it for *Live In Japan* (1992).
* "Run Of The Mill." This statement of personal responsibility, on *All Things Must Pass* (1970), is about conflict within The Beatles. See 154.
* "Sat Singing." Although this is a crucial song for interpreting George's religiosity, it's not well known. Originally a contribution to *Somewhere In England* (1981), it was among the songs pulled to please the record producers, who rejected George's original project. It later showed up on *Songs By George Harrison* (1989), which is all but impossible to obtain. Fans know it primarily through bootlegs. Its obscurity is unfortunate. Not only do the words document an important mystical experience, when George's self-consciousness took a holiday and he felt himself becoming one with God, but the music itself is well done and features fine guitar solos. See 8, 10, 17, 18, 74, 121, 122, 125, 126, 132, 134.
* "Save The World." A litany of ecological complaint, set to idiosyncratic music seemingly influenced by *Monty Python's Flying Circus*.

There is one version on *Somewhere In England* (1989), another on *Greenpeace: The Album* (1985). Although the sentiments seem clichéd—the rain forest is getting chopped down, the whales are being slaughtered, nuclear power will cause cancer, etc.—George recorded this song several times and put it on two different albums, so clearly he took its message seriously. See 70, 75, 77n.6, 87, 99.

* "Savoy Truffle." One of George's contributions to *The Beatles (The White Album)* (1968), this is about nothing more than Eric Clapton's sweet tooth for candies. Most of the words can be found on the candy box pictured on plate XXII of Harrison, *I, Me, Mine*.
* "See Yourself." A call to serious self-examination from *Thirty-Three & 1/3* (1976), it recalls the earlier and better "Run Of The Mill." The story behind the song, which contains George's reflections on Paul's public admission that he had taken LSD, is in Harrison, *I, Me, Mine*, 108. See 118, 125.
* "Shanghai Surprise." Until this showed up as a bonus track on the recent rerelease of *Cloud Nine*, the song was available only on bootlegs. George composed the piece for the failed movie *Shanghai Surprise*. See 102. It has no religious import.
* "Simply Shady." This is the second entry on *Dark Horse* (1974). Harrison, in *I, Me, Mine*, 282, says it concerns "what happens to naughty boys in the music business." The song is of religious interest because of its strong statement that we cannot avoid the effects of our actions and because of its indictment of George's behavior, above all his craving. See 62, 64, 87, 94n.2, 100, 120, 129.
* "Singing Om." An instrumental piece on *Wonderwall* (1968). See 122.
* "Ski-ing." Another instrumental for *Wonderwall* (1968).
* "So Sad." This is, according to *I, Me, Mine*, 240, a testimony to how George felt during his breakup with his first wife, Pattie: their marriage had turned to stone and then crumbled at his feet. The song, written while George was staying alone in a New York hotel, appears on *Dark Horse* (1974). See 118.
* "Soft-Hearted Hana." This contribution to *George Harrison* (1979), with its upbeat, bluegrass sound, is nearly unintelligible. According to George himself, the words recount a 1978 trip on magic mushrooms and are "a bit crazy" (*I, Me, Mine*, 351). The song seems more

than anything else a record of drug-induced images and recalls The Beatles' "I Am The Walrus." "Hana" is the section of Maui on which George had his Hawaiian estate.

* "Soft Touch." Written in the Virgin Islands, this is a secular love song on *George Harrison* (1979). See 12.
* "Someplace Else." Originally composed for the movie *Shanghai Surprise*, this later showed up on *Cloud Nine* (1987). It's an effective expression of alienation from the world. See 108, 118. It would have been more at home on *Extra Texture: Read All About It* than the jaunty *Cloud Nine*.
* "Something." George's famous love song, from *Abbey Road* (1969). It seems to be about human, not divine love, and Pattie Harrison once said George was thinking of her when he wrote it. But there are Hare Krishna devotees who report George's saying to them, "Actually, it's about Krishna. But I couldn't say 'he,' could I? I had to say 'she' or they'd think I'm a poof."[1] Live versions are on *Concert For Bangladesh* (1971) and *Live In Japan* (1992). It's also on The Beatles' *Anthology 3* (1996). As a way of honoring George, both Paul McCartney and Bob Dylan sang "Something" in concerts shortly after their friend's death. Next to "Yesterday," it's the most covered song of The Beatles. See 132.
* "Sour Milk Sea." George gave this rocker to Jackie Lomax, and it's on the latter's *Is This What You Want?* (1969), an album with the Apple label. The song features George and Eric Clapton on guitar, Ringo on drums, and Paul on bass, yet unaccountably never climbed the charts. It promotes Transcendental Meditation. See 45.
* "Sri Ishopanishad." A four-minute entry on *Chant And Be Happy* (1991).
* "Sri Guruvastakam." The shortest song on *Chant And Be Happy* (1991).
* "Stuck Inside A Cloud." Clearly the product of a personal crisis, this expresses George's desire to touch the "lotus feet" of an unidentified "you." It's on *Brainwashed* (2002), which in its entirety expresses a good deal of anxiety. See 21, 75, 103, 110, 117, 143.
* "Sue Me, Sue You Blues." This is the second entry on *Living In The Material World* (1973). George uses his slide to good effect here in bitterly recounting the lawsuits that followed the breakup of The

Beatles. The demo version exists on bootlegs and is worth hearing as George sounds just like an old Delta Blues guitarist. The song has no religious message. See 36, 112n.1, 132.

- "Tabla And Pakavaj." An instrumental on *Wonderwall* (1968). A tabla is a small Indian drum. A pakavaj is another Indian percussion instrument. Both are played on *Wonderwall*.
- "Tandoori Chicken." An unimportant song George wrote for Ronnie Spector in a Carl Perkins style. It was the B-side to "Try Some Buy Some" (1971) and got no more airplay than the latter.
- "Taxman." George's complaint about paying too much to the British government; it opens *Revolver* (1966). Other versions may be found on *The Concert For Bangladesh* (1971), *Live In Japan* (1992), and The Beatles' *Anthology 3* (1996). See 102, 133, 145, 158.
- "Teardrops." A jaunty tune on *Somewhere In England* (1989) that doesn't seem to say much. It failed as a single.
- "Tears Of The World." An outtake from *Somewhere In England*, this appeared on *Songs by George Harrison: Volume 2* (1992) and fortunately later became a bonus track on the reissued CD of *Thirty-Three & 1/3*. See 56, 70, 129, 131n.8, 132.
- "Thanks For The Pepperoni." An instrumental jam session on *All Things Must Pass* (1970) which works with guitar riffs from the 1950s.
- "That Is All." The conclusion to *Living In The Material World* (1973). This is presumably a love song to a woman, not God, although with George one never knows for sure. The theme of words falling short is central. See 124.
- "That Kind Of Woman." Although George wrote this lyrically innocuous love song, Eric Clapton did it for *Nobody's Child: Romanian Angel Appeal* (1990).
- "That Which I Have Lost." *Somewhere In England* (1989) contains "Unconsciousness Rules," which disparages those who behave in a juvenile fashion. Its counterpart is "That Which I Have Lost," which revels in the enlightenment that illuminates the consciousness. George himself said that the song, which is about overcoming darkness and limitation, comes straight out of the *Bhagavad-Gita*. See 19, 62, 63, 72, 80, 83, 86, 90, 97, 98, 112, 118, 120, 128, 129, 130, 143.

* "That's The Way It Goes." One of the better songs on *Gone Troppo* (1982), which Joe Brown reprised wonderfully for *The Concert For George* (2003). The message is plain: spiritual things matter; material things don't. See 76, 97, 117, 120, 125, 132.
* "That's What It Takes." George wrote this *Cloud Nine* (1987) number with Jeff Lynne and Gary Wright. The lyrics seem to offer a cryptic version of "The Art Of Dying": one needs to work in preparation for the shining world beyond death. See 80, 128.
* "Think For Yourself." In *I, Me, Mine*, 88, George fails to remember what exactly this number on *Rubber Soul* (1965) is about.
* "This Guitar (Can't Keep From Crying)." Appearing on *Extra Texture: Read All About It* (1975), this beautiful song, with its ardent lyrics, deserves to be better known. Released as a single, it went nowhere on the charts. It records George's deep hurt in response to criticisms of his 1974 North American tour. See 132.
* "This Is Love." A paean to love and self-help written with Jeff Lynne for *Cloud Nine* (1987). See 74, 97, 126.
* "This Song." The comic relief on *Thirty-Three & 1/3* (1976), this is George's response to the famous lawsuit over "My Sweet Lord." The single made it to number fifteen on the American Billboard chart. The accompanying madcap video is now available on *The Dark Horse Years 1976–1992* (2004). Ironically, the opening sounds a bit like The Four Tops' "I Can't Help Myself (Sugar Pie, Honey Bunch)." See 36, 133.
* "Tired Of Midnight Blue." One of the best songs on *Extra Texture: Read All About It* (1975), it seems to record disillusionment with George's so-called "naughty period" of 1974 and all it stood for. In hindsight, George would now rather be at home than out partying.
* "True Love." A cover of an old Cole Porter song on *Thirty Three & 1/3* (1976).
* "Try Some Buy Some." Written originally for Ronnie Spector in 1971, who didn't understand the song at all and sang it accordingly, this is yet another love song about God, on *Living In The Material World* (1973). George is contrasting life without God to life with God. See 19, 100, 104, 113, 156.
* "Unconsciousness Rules." Musically happy but lyrically discourteous, this song on 1981's *Somewhere In England* is a rant against the

disco craze. The accusation of unconsciousness means that those in love with the nightlife of the discothèque are self-centered ("ego'd out") and full of misplaced desire. See 33, 34, 57, 61, 66, 85, 98, 99, 156.

* "Under The Mersey Wall." A wildly unsuccessful attempt to produce *Electronic Sound* (1969). It occupies one whole side of the album. Unfortunately, the other side is just as miserably boring.

* "Unknown Delight." A love song to George's son, Dhani, on *Gone Troppo* (1982). See 11, 65.

* "Wah-Wah." George wrote this catchy song during the filming of *Let It Be*, after becoming annoyed with both Paul and Yoko Ono. George later said that "Wah-Wah" in effect means "headache." But as he is referring to the wah-wah guitar pedal, and as Vox had, by 1968, produced their Crybaby model, there may be additional connotations. The song appears on *All Things Must Pass* (1970), and there is a live version on *The Concert For Bangladesh* (1971).

* "Wake Up My Love." On *Gone Troppo* (1982), this can be understood to be about George's relationship with God or his wife or perhaps both at the same time. I prefer the religious reading: George is asking for spiritual renewal, praying that he might feel God again as he did in the past. See 12, 117, 128.

* "What Is Life." An agreeable pop song for *All Things Must Pass* (1970); it probably has no theological content. Alternate versions are on *Live In Japan* (1992) and on the remastered *All Things Must Pass* (2001). See 124, 132.

* "When We Was Fab." Written with Jeff Lynne for *Cloud Nine* (1987), the music recalls "I Am The Walrus" while the words are an ambiguous reflection on George's time as a Beatle. There are also references to Frank Sinatra's "Strangers In The Night," George's "Taxman," Dylan's "It's All Over Now, Baby Blue," and Smokey Robinson's "You Really Got A Hold On Me." The amusing video, which has Ringo on drums and Paul in a Walrus suit, is now easily accessible on *The Dark Horse Years 1976–1992* (2004). See 9, 85, 89, 160.

* "While My Guitar Gently Weeps." This was one of the highlights of *The Beatles (The White Album)* (1968) and has not lost its charm over the years. It conveys spiritual angst and an urgently religious point of view without being explicitly theological. The live version of this

on the *The Concert For Bangladesh* (1971) features a weak performance by Clapton. His rendition on *Live In Japan* (1992) is much more interesting, but his best performance is on *The Concert For George* (2003). The Beatles' *Anthology 3* (1996) preserves a demo. See 2, 67, 70, 132.

- "Who Can See It." This piece to *Living In The Material World* (1973) seems to be George's bitter reflection on his past as a Beatle, how he was "held up" and "run down." Here he declares his freedom from his past, his freedom to be himself. See 34, 117.

- "Within You Without You." One of George's early statements of his spirituality, although explicitly theological statements are absent. It's on *Sgt. Pepper's Lonely Hearts Club Band* (1967). George's later interpretation of the song is clear from his public comments after Roy Orbison's death: "He's out there, really, his spirit. You know, life flows on within you and without you. He's around." See 29, 57, 64, 74, 79, 86, 96, 120.

- "Woman Don't You Cry For Me." Although on *Thirty-Three & 1/3* (1976), George commenced work on this in 1968, when he was learning to play slide guitar. It's a song of farewell to a woman, but it nevertheless manages to say two things dear to George's philosophy: attachment to anything in this world is harmful, and all that matters is God. See 27, 120.

- "Wonderwall To Be Here." An instrumental piece on *Wonderwall* (1968).

- "World of Stone." An expression of alienation from the world on *Extra Texture: Read All About It* (1975). It warns others not to make George an idol or to emulate him, and its sad last line articulates George's felt distance from God: he is far "from OM." See 7, 118, 122.

- "Wrack My Brain." This expresses frustrated resignation in the face of a failed relationship. George never recorded it himself but gave it to Ringo Starr, who released it as a single in 1981. It also appears on Ringo's *Stop And Smell The Roses* (1981). George produced the song, sang in the background, and played guitar. See 100.

- "Wreck Of The Hesperus." A humorous response to aging, the poisonous press, empty fame, and gossip, on *Cloud Nine* (1987). The

repeated conclusion, "It's alright," is for George a cosmic generalization. See 9, 36, 38, 93, 116.
- "Writing's On The Wall." A musically idiosyncratic contribution to *Somewhere In England* (1989). It's almost a précis of George's spirituality: we should live in the light of death; God dwells inside us all; music can bring spiritual healing; we need to cultivate love. See 57, 62, 80, 100, 129.
- "You." The opening entry on *Extra Texture: Read All About It* (1975), it was originally written for Ronnie Spector, of The Ronettes fame. She never used this secular love song, for which George had already done the instrumentals in 1970. For George it was a hit. See 137.
- "You And Me (Babe)." Written with Mal Evans and recorded by Ringo for his 1973 album, *Ringo*. It's of no lyrical significance. See 100.
- "You Know What To Do." George's second composition for The Beatles, it was never finished, and the demo didn't appear until *Anthology 1* (1995). It's a juvenile love song, lyrically arid.
- "You Like Me Too Much." A simple love song from *Help!* (1965).
- "Your Love Is Forever." One can ask whether this is about Olivia or God or both. The words near the end, "the only lover worth it all," tip the scale in favor of a religious reading, and in an interview George himself said it means the same thing as "My Sweet Lord." The song is on *George Harrison* (1979). George's comments in *I, Me, Mine*, 362, concern the music, not the lyrics. See 11, 90, 127.
- "Zig Zag." Written with Jeff Lynne, this is the forgettable B-side of "When We Was Fab." It can be heard on the soundtrack of the dismal *Shanghai Surprise* and as a bonus on the recent reissue of *Cloud Nine*. The lyrics only repeat the title, so the song is meaningless.

Note

1. Joshua M. Greene, *Here Comes The Sun: The Spiritual and Musical Journey of George Harrison* (Hoboken, NJ: John Wiley & Sons, 2006), 142.

Index

Abbey Road, 2, 45, 144, 155
"After The Gold Rush," 71
Afterlife, 14, 51, 67, 78–94, 134, 135
   See also Heaven, Hell, and Reincarnation
Albert, Herb, 148
Alcohol, 99, 100, 102, 148
Alcoholics Anonymous (AA), 100, 148
Alienation, 34, 97, 99, 103, 152
All Things Must Pass, 2, 6, 8, 37, 42, 46–48, 63, 66, 71, 84, 91, 100, 108, 122, 135–37, 139, 142, 144–48, 150, 152, 153, 156, 158
"All You Need Is Love," 13, 127, 134
Allah, 60
Alpert, Richard, 23
"And Your Bird Can Sing," 31
Apple, 72, 46, 116, 136, 151, 155
Apple Scruffs, 136
Arjuna, 29, 107
Arlen, Harold, 137
Armstrong, Louis, 140
Atkins, Susan, 98
Atman, 120
Attachment, 28, 32, 62, 63, 65, 84, 92, 114, 119, 120, 127, 159
Autobiography Of A Yogi, 49, 60, 76, 89, 94, 101, 112, 140

"Ballad Of John And Yoko," 118, 151
Banking, 41, 99
Barham, John, 148

Beatles, The, 1, 2, 5, 9, 12, 18, 19, 22, 23, 26, 31, 35, 36, 42–46, 50, 51, 53, 57, 60, 66, 67, 70, 72–74, 81, 95, 97, 100–102, 107, 108, 112, 112, 119, 133, 135, 136, 139–41, 144, 146–56, 158–60
The Beatles' Anthology (3 vols.), 57, 60, 67, 119, 135, 139, 140, 147, 152, 155, 156, 159, 160
The Beatles' Past Masters, Vol. 2, 26, 147
The Beatles' Rarities, 147
The Beatles (The White Album), 2, 12, 19, 45, 70, 72, 97, 149, 151, 152, 154, 158
Bedford, Carol, 136
Bee Gees, The, 69
Be Here Now, 84–85, 137
Berry, Chuck, 153
Best of Dark Horse, 138, 139, 152
Best of George Harrison, 142
Bhagavad-Gita, 7, 11, 19, 26, 29, 31, 47, 51, 66, 73, 106, 107, 119, 126, 127, 129, 131, 156
Bhakti, 11, 12, 125, 126
Bible, 9, 11, 33, 51, 56–58, 60, 64, 71, 76, 88, 92, 101, 121, 146, 148, 149
Big Business, 66, 70–73, 98, 99, 138
Blake, William, 31, 97
Blavatsky, Madame, 43
Bliss, 7, 8, 10, 17, 21, 48, 80, 84, 90, 91, 94, 109, 127, 129

Bob Dylan, 81
Bowie, David, 113
Boyd, Pattie, 7, 44, 138, 154, 155
Brahman, 7, 11, 90, 120, 122
Brahmo, 73
Brainwashed, 2, 6, 21, 29, 33, 41, 42, 46, 48, 56, 70, 71, 99, 108, 109, 111, 123, 125, 128, 131, 136–38, 149, 150–53, 155
Brown, Joe, 4, 157
Bruce, Lenny, 36
Bryant, Felice and Boodleaux, 138
Buckley, Lord, 29
Buddha, 51, 52, 55, 60, 62, 149
Bunbury Tales, 153
Byrds, The, 23, 44

Carmichael, Hoagie, 137, 145
Cashmere, Paul, 39
Catholicism, *see* Roman Catholic Church
Ceausescu, Nicolae, 69
Chanting, 7, 33, 42–44, 46–49, 59, 122–124, 127, 143, 144, 147
   See also Hare Krishna Mantra and Mantra
Chants of India, 44, 123, 136
Chiffons, The, 36
Chopra, Deepak, 14, 60, 94
Christianity, 3, 15, 28, 29, 32, 40, 42, 49, 50, 53–56, 58, 60, 62, 68, 73, 87, 99, 102, 133, 145, 151
   See also Bible, Jesus Christ, and Roman Catholic Church
Clapton, Eric, 2, 4, 9, 32, 35, 69, 92, 100, 116, 136, 138, 144, 154–56, 159
Clark, Rudy, 143
Clayson, Alan, 5, 22
Cloud Nine, 9, 20, 37, 41, 48, 101, 112, 138–41, 143, 148, 152, 154, 155–60

Coben, Cy, 151
Coltrane, John, 59
Concert for Bangladesh, 13, 68, 69
Concert for Bangladesh, The, 35, 69, 136, 137, 144, 147, 150, 155, 156, 158, 159
Concert for George, The, 4, 36, 44, 152, 155, 157, 159
Consciousness, 14, 15, 19, 22, 27, 28, 45, 48, 62, 74, 98, 104, 106, 112, 115, 120, 125, 127, 130, 149, 153, 156
Conversion experience, 15–17, 20–22, 103–5, 108, 115
Coulter, John, 148
Crawdaddy, 22, 23
Cream, 136
Creed, 3
Creedence Clearwater Revival, 79
Creem, 23, 77, 112
Crisp, Frank, 63, 135, 136, 142
Crosby, David, 44

Dark Horse, 46–48, 65, 71, 122, 138–41, 144, 147, 150, 152, 154
Dark Horse Years, The, 29, 55, 70, 139–41, 143, 157, 158
Darkness, 19, 27, 34, 66, 67, 87, 88, 90, 105, 112, 125, 126, 130, 156
Davies, Ray, 27
"A Day In The Life," 31, 101
Death and Dying, 7–9, 14, 18, 21, 23, 24, 25, 27, 28, 32, 46, 54, 56, 62, 69, 78–94, 103, 104, 109, 134, 140, 144, 148–50, 152, 153, 157, 159, 160
Depression, 7, 19, 81, 118, 143
Desire, 6, 32, 33, 62–64, 80, 84, 93, 117–20, 123, 124, 127, 129–31, 143, 158
Despair, 10, 116, 118, 143, 146
Devi, Indra, 43

Index

Devil, The, 54, 99–102, 110
Disco music, 33, 100, 158
Dissatisfaction with Life or World, 115–20
Double Fantasy, 53
Down In The Groove, 81
Dream, Life as, 18, 27, 32, 65, 66, 83, 84
Duality and Opposition, 11, 63, 83, 84, 105, 136, 141
Dylan, Bob, 4, 29, 37, 52, 69, 72, 81, 89, 133 137, 145, 146, 155, 158

Eckhart, Meister, 30
Egoism, 30, 31, 46, 98, 114, 119, 146, 158
Eighties, The (1980s), 2, 59, 138
Einstein, Albert, 89
"Eleanor Rigby," 50, 81
Electronic Sound, 22, 151, 158
Elvis Presley, 142
Enlightenment, 46, 62, 67, 83, 90, 92, 96, 107, 98, 103, 105, 123, 128, 133, 156
Environment, 32, 69–71, 75, 98, 139, 154. *See also* Nature
Epic Of Gilgamesh, 87
Evans, Mal, 100, 160
Everly Brothers, 138
Evil, Problem of, 12–14
Extra Texture: Read All About It, 7, 8, 10, 11, 84, 122, 135, 137, 138, 140, 143, 144, 152, 155, 157, 159, 160
"Eye To Eye," 73

Fame, 44, 49, 57, 85, 102, 116, 117, 119, 120, 141, 148, 159
Fiddler on the Roof, 9
"Fixin' To Die Blues," 81
Fogerty, John, 79

Foree, Mel, 151
Forgiveness, 108, 144
Four Tops, The, 157
Freud, Sigmund, 14
Friar Park Mansion, 35, 108, 135, 136, 140
Friendship, 62, 117
Frost, David, 38

Gandhi, Mahatma, 43
Gardening, 4, 35, 71
George Harrison, 11, 48, 71, 102, 138, 140, 141, 144, 146, 149, 151, 154, 155, 160
"Get Back," 135
Gilliam, Terry, 2
Gilmour, Michael J., 131
Ginsberg, Allen, 59
Giuliano, Geoffrey, 23, 59
God, 6–23, 28–30, 32, 33, 35, 37, 42, 44, 47–57, 60, 62, 63, 65, 67, 72, 74, 76, 78, 80, 84, 86, 88–91, 93, 94, 97, 101–6, 108–11, 115, 117, 120–30, 133–36, 138, 140, 141, 143–49, 151, 153, 156–60. *See also* Grace of God and Union with God
God Realization, 48, 54, 120, 121, 122, 145
Gone Troppo, 48, 71, 76, 82, 117, 136, 139, 141–44, 146, 151, 157, 158
Goodbye, 136
Gospels, 33, 50, 56–58, 106, 121, 149
Gossip, 98, 99, 140, 159
Gosvami, Rupa, 123
Goswami, Mukunda, 22, 23, 39, 47, 59, 60, 64, 94, 112, 113, 131
Grace of God, 19, 37, 64, 115, 129–30, 149
"The Great Wok," 52
Greene, Joshua M., 5, 112, 160
Greenpeace, 71, 154
Greif, George, 39

"Grow Old With Me," 53
Gunn, Kevin, 23

Hallelujah, 46, 55, 60
Hare Krishnas, 16, 45–47, 51, 56, 59, 123, 143, 155
Hare Krishna Mantra, 46, 47, 122, 142, 144, 153
Harrison, Dhani, 11, 47, 65, 158
Harrison, Harry, 17, 23, 40
Harrison, Louise, 17, 40, 58, 89, 140
Harrison, Olivia, 31, 69, 94, 137, 140, 151, 160
Heart, 3, 8, 15, 17, 22, 28, 29, 49, 54, 56, 70, 107, 118, 123, 125, 133, 136, 141, 143, 149
Heaven, 19, 27, 29, 51, 68, 80, 82, 87, 89, 90, 91. *See also* Higher World and Spiritual Sky
Hell, 51, 75, 87, 107
Help!, 43, 44, 146, 160
"Help Me To Help Myself," 53, 54
Henley, Don, 100
"He's So Fine," 36
Hey Jude, 151
Higher World, 63, 80, 82, 84, 87, 90–92, 127. *See also* Heaven and Spiritual Sky
"Highway 51 Blues," 81
Highway 51 Revisited, 81
Hinduism, 3, 10, 11, 26, 30, 35, 43, 44, 48, 50, 51, 55, 64, 72, 73, 81, 87, 106, 119, 120, 127, 151
Holland, Jools, 54, 93, 145
"How Do You Sleep?," 97
Humanitarianism, 13, 68–76, 134, 137, 141, 151
Huntley, Elliot J., 5, 60
Huxley, Aldous, 30, 31, 39, 43, 97

"I Am The Walrus," 46, 51, 155, 158

"I Can't Help Myself (Sugar Pie, Honey Bunch)," 157
"I Found Out," 51
I, Me, Mine, by George Harrison, 5, 22, 23, 31, 38, 39, 59, 60, 91, 94, 105, 107, 119, 131, 136, 138, 139, 145, 148, 150, 151, 154, 157, 160
"I Saw Her Standing There," 1
"I Want To Hold Your Hand," 1
Idle, Eric, 36
Ignorance, 29, 32, 34, 65, 67, 97, 101, 106–7, 110, 120
Iliad, The, 87
"Imagine," 51–53
India and Indian Music, 2, 11, 17, 32, 43–47, 51, 56–59, 64, 73, 107, 117, 119, 137, 140, 147, 156
"In My Life," 81, 147
"In My Time Of Dyin'," 81
"Instant Karma," 45, 83
International Society of Krishna Consciousness (ISKCON), *see* Hare Krishnas
Introversion, 3, 35, 107, 147
"It's All Over Now Baby Blue," 158

James, William, 103, 104, 112
Japa, 7, 58, 131
Jehovah, 55
Jesus Christ, 37, 51, 52, 54–58, 60, 68, 121, 136, 148, 149
John, Elton, 9, 69
John Lennon Anthology, 51, 53
Journeyman, 138
Judgment at Death, 86–87, 149
Julian of Norwich, 38

Kafka, Franz, 67
Karma, 45, 46, 54, 60, 62, 80, 83, 86, 87, 89, 94, 97, 127, 129, 149
The Kinks, 27, 58, 59

Koehler, Ted, 137
Krishna, 7, 9, 10, 12, 15, 21, 22, 29, 30, 46–49, 51, 52, 55, 56, 58, 60, 64, 106, 107, 122, 124, 125, 130, 142–44, 147, 149, 155
Krshna: The Supreme Personality of the Godhead, 22, 23, 39, 46, 60

"Lady Madonna," 26, 147
Lauda, Niki, 102
Law, William, 28
Leary, Timothy, 14, 16, 23, 30, 85, 135
Leng, Simon, 5, 77
Lennon, John, 13, 16, 43–46, 50–54, 59, 60, 64, 72, 88, 95, 98, 100, 108, 118, 135, 139, 147, 148, 151 *See also* The Beatles
Lethal Weapon 2, 138
Let It Be, 31, 142, 146, 158
Life of Brian, 2, 60
Light, 12, 17–19, 22, 23, 27, 29, 30, 34, 52, 63, 66, 67, 74, 80, 83, 87–91, 94, 99, 101, 102, 105, 106, 112, 125, 128, 130, 133, 140, 142, 149, 160
Live In Japan, 35, 135, 138, 139, 140–44, 146, 147, 150–52, 155, 156, 158, 159
Living In The Material World, 8, 19, 21, 22, 37, 42, 47, 48, 61–77, 84, 122, 137, 140–42, 150, 155–57, 159
Lomax, Jackie, 45, 155
Loneliness, 19, 81, 118
Longfellow, Henry Wadsworth, 9
Lotus feet, 21, 110, 143, 155
Love, 11–12, 28, 38, 49, 52, 53, 64, 65, 70, 72, 73, 79, 88, 89, 94, 96, 97, 104, 110–12, 121, 125–28, 130, 134, 136–38, 140–42, 145–49, 151–53, 155–58, 160

LSD, 16, 20, 23, 26, 28, 30, 85, 103, 115, 144, 154
Lynne, Jeff, 4, 157, 158, 160

McCartney, Linda, 135
McCartney, Paul, 4, 5, 35, 36, 37, 44, 45, 59, 64, 97, 112, 135, 147, 151, 154, 155, 158. *See also* The Beatles
McGuinn, Roger, 23, 44
Mack, Ronald, 36
Madonna, 26, 147
Magical Mystery Tour, 26, 46, 138, 147
Maharishi Mahesh Yogi, 11, 38, 44, 45–46, 51, 53, 73, 119
"Man Of Constant Sorrow," 81, 89
Manson, Charles, 98
Mantra, 46–48, 52, 122, 142, 144
Martin, Bill, 148
Marx, Karl, 14, 68
Mascaró, Juan, 38
Material World, 25, 27, 28, 31, 32, 34, 35, 61–77, 80, 82–85, 87, 90–93, 106, 110, 111, 114, 115, 118, 122, 123, 125, 127, 133, 134, 137
mâya (illusion), 8, 11, 32, 34, 37, 63–68, 72, 74, 83, 85, 92, 101, 106–7, 110, 111, 115, 128, 137, 140, 150
Media, The, 99, 100, 101, 102, 112, 159
Meditation, 11, 15, 16, 18, 31, 44, 45, 49, 58, 59, 65, 75, 119, 125, 155
Meet The Beatles, 141
Melody Maker, 22
Menken, H. L., 36
Mercer, Johnny, 19
Metzner, Ralph, 23
Michelangelo, 41
Milk and Honey, 53
Mister Roadrunner, 137

Modern Technology, 7, 70, 99
Moksha, 37, 87
Monty Python, 2, 36, 60, 70, 153
Moon, *see* Sun
Moore, Charles, 77
Morrison, Van, 69
Muhammed, 52, 55
Mysticism/mystical experience, 17–19, 30, 90, 91, 121, 122, 125, 153

Natural Law Party, 45, 75
Nature, 70–76, 82, 104, 134, 144, 148. *See also* Environment and Sun and Moon
Near Death Experience, 18, 89
Nietzsche, Friedrich, 14
Nineties (1990s), 36, 138
Nobody's Child: Roman Angel Appeal, 69, 151, 156
"Norwegian Wood," 44
Nuclear Power, 70–71, 75, 154

OM, 7, 122, 142, 154, 159
Ono, Yoko, 45, 53, 554, 59, 118, 151, 158
Optimism, 76, 38, 67, 75, 103, 138, 149
Orbison, Roy, 142, 144, 151, 159
Ostin, Mo, 137, 150

Palin, Michael, 36
Partying, 4, 33, 85, 99–100, 102, 157
Pascal, Blaise, 33, 62
Past Masters, 26, 147
Pat Garrett And Billy The Kid, 81
"Penny Lane," 27
Perception and Misperception, 15, 16, 18, 20, 22, 24, 32, 63–66, 83, 90, 91, 95–97, 103–7, 117, 120, 122, 125, 128. *See also maya*
Perkins, Carl, 142, 156

Pessimism, 76, 96, 103, 107
Petty, Tom, 4, 138
Pisces, Sign of, 10, 109, 152
Plato, 28, 91
Polanski, Roman, 98
Politics, 41, 45, 53, 66, 70, 72, 75, 76, 99, 139, 156
Pope, The, 42, 76, 152
Porky's Revenge, 145
Porter, Cole, 157
Prabhavananda, Swami, 11, 43, 55
Prabhupada, Swami, 22, 39, 45, 56
Prayer, 6, 41, 49, 52, 53, 58, 79, 82, 84, 89, 90, 101, 108, 109, 120, 124, 125, 130, 134, 136, 140, 142, 146, 153, 158
Prayer beads, 42, 58, 136
Preston, Billy, 69
"Prisoner, The," 37

Race Car Driving, 102, 103, 112, 141
Radha, 127
Radhakrishnan, 15, 23, 77
"Rain," 31, 95, 96
Ram Das, 85, 137
Ray, James, 9, 143
Reincarnation, 28, 54, 78–94, 118, 127, 128, 130, 136, 139, 142
Relphs, Mick, 142
Revolver, 18, 26, 44, 146, 150, 156
Richards, Cliff, 148
Rig Veda, 55
Ringo, 71, 100, 152, 160
Ringo Rama, 73, 83
Ringo's Rotogravure, 37, 147
"The Rishi Kesh Song," 52
Robinson, Smokey, 152, 153, 158
Rolling Stone, 2, 67, 113
Rolling Stones, The, 149
Roman Catholic Church, 3, 17, 33, 40–42, 50, 54, 58, 56, 62, 94, 99, 152

Romanian Angels Appeal, 13, 69, 151, 156
Ronettes, The, 160
Rosen, Robert, 59
Rubber Soul, 44, 58, 146, 157
Russell, Leon, 69
Ruttles, The, 36

Sai Baba, Sathya, 11, 53
Salvation, 28, 37–38, 67, 68, 104, 114–31, 149
Seaman, Frederic, 60
"See That My Grave's Kept Clean," 81
Self-Realization Fellowship, 17, 49
Sellers, Peter, 36
Senses, The Physical, 25, 32, 61–63, 65, 91, 118, 125, 149
Sgt. Pepper's Lonely Hearts Club Band, 49, 64, 151, 159
"Serve Yourself," 51, 52
Seventies, The (1970s), 2, 7, 19, 33, 35, 36, 48, 53, 71, 100, 102, 136, 138, 144
"Sexy Sadie," 51
Shanghai Surprise, 102, 138, 145, 154, 155, 160
Shankara, 11
Shankar, Anoushka, 4, 44
Shankar, Ravi, 2, 44, 59, 68, 123, 136
Silence, 26, 101, 124, 125
"Silvio," 81
Simon, Paul, 69
Sinatra, Frank, 158
Sistine Chapel, 41, 76
Sitar, 2, 26, 43–44, 58, 59, 150
Sixties (1960s), 19, 20. 26, 29, 42, 43, 48, 70, 72–75, 97, 99, 112, 115, 120, 133, 140, 142, 145
Small World, Big Band, 54, 93, 145
Smith, Legs Larry, 144
Somach, Denny, 23
Somach, Kathleen, 23

Somewhere In England, 8, 17, 27, 48, 61, 62, 70, 71, 85, 98, 135, 137, 145, 148, 153, 154, 156, 157, 160
Songs of George Harrison (vols. 1 & 2), 17, 142, 144, 145, 148, 149, 153, 164
Soul, 22, 24, 23, 26, 27, 29, 30, 34, 67, 80, 82, 88, 105, 109, 111, 119, 121, 131, 134
Spector, Ronie, 113, 156, 157, 160
Spiritual Eye, 97, 117, 125
Spiritual Sky, 64, 130. *See also* Heaven and Higher World
Starr, Ringo, 4, 36, 37, 43–45, 59, 64, 69, 71, 73, 83, 100, 135, 147, 151, 152, 155, 158–60. *See also* The Beatles
Stations of the Cross, 40
Stereos, The, 146
Stewart, Jackie, 102, 141
Stop And Smell The Roses, 159
"Strangers In The Night," 158
"Strawberry Fields Forever," 27
Sufism, 10
Suicide, 7, 22, 78, 80, 143
Sullivan, Ed, 1, 139
Sun and Moon, 11, 17, 18, 28, 30, 71, 74, 88, 90, 95, 96, 99, 110, 144
Swearingen, Leroy, 146

Tagore, Rabindranath, 43
Tao Te Ching, 26, 27, 38, 135, 147
Tate, Sharon, 98
Taylor, Derek, 23, 113, 72
Television, 99, 101, 102
Tennyson, Alfred Lord, 88
Thirty Three & 1/3, 8, 36, 49, 137, 139, 140, 148, 153, 154, 156, 157, 159
Three Dog Night, 71
Time Bandits, 2, 65, 141
"Tombstone Blues," 81

"Tomorrow Never Knows," 23, 31
Transience, 26, 62, 63, 65, 79, 81, 115, 117, 152
The Traveling Wilburys, 2, 18, 19, 69, 88, 141, 143, 144, 150
The Traveling Wilburys, Vol. 1, 141, 143, 144
The Traveling Wilburys, Vol. 3, 150
Transcendental Meditation (TM), 11, 31, 44, 45, 75, 119, 155
"Twice-born, The," 19, 103–6, 111

U 2, 3
Unconsciousness, 32, 33, 36, 66, 85, 122, 137, 156–58
Union with God, 11, 30, 31, 87, 115, 120–22, 127
Unity of All, 30, 63, 64, 83, 84, 97
Upanishads, 32
Utopia, 51, 62–63, 73, 140, 141

Vatican, 41, 42
Vedanta, 11, 43, 55
Vedic Scriptures, 55, 63, 123

Vishnu, 46, 149
Vishnu-devananda, Swami, 43
Vishnu Purana, 57

"Walk On The Water," 79
War, 71–73, 80, 98, 99
Wealth, 7, 30, 61, 88, 97–99, 107, 117, 119
With The Beatles, 141, 157
Wonder, Stevie, 69
Wonderwall, 22, 122, 139, 141–43, 147, 150–54, 156, 159
Wood, Ronnie, 141
Wright, Gary, 157

Yellow Submarine, 147, 151
Yin and Yang, 83
Yoga, 16, 43, 51, 56, 125, 131
Yogananda, Paramahansa, 17, 48, 49, 56, 60, 76, 88, 89, 90, 94, 101, 112, 140
Yogoda Satsanga Society, 17
"You Really Got A Hold Of Me," 158
Young, Neil, 71

www.ingramcontent.com/pod-product-compliance
Lightning Source LLC
Chambersburg PA
CBHW051812230426
43672CB00012B/2707